March 24, 2005
Robert C [illegible]

The Saga of a Vietnamese Immigrant

by

Robert C. Trando
(aka Tran-do Cung)

authorHOUSE

1663 Liberty Drive, Suite 200
Bloomington, Indiana 47403
(800) 839-8640
www.authorhouse.com

First published by AuthorHouse 08/03/04

ISBN: 1-4184-7551-3 (e)
ISBN: 1-4184-7550-5 (sc)

Library of Congress Control Number: 2004095211

Printed in the United States of America
Bloomington, Indiana

This book is printed on acid-free paper.

TABLE OF CONTENTS

To my parents, parents-in-law, my wife, siblings, children and grand children

FOREWORD

After selling my business and retiring in 1997 I had spent a few years traveling with my wife. We went back to France and then we went on a 21 day trip arranged by Grand Circle Travel to China to see the marvels of that old country .Then we wanted to really settle down enjoying the few grandchildren who are still around us. I decided to write my memoir in Vietnamese trying to put on paper my recollection of my past with the desire to let my kids and also my wife know of all of the things I have been through or witnessed.

To my amazement so many things that lay deep in my sub conscience suddenly awakened and as the French say "de fil a aiguille", or from thread to needle, all the data randomly appeared and became organized as I went along sitting in front of my word processor. So I finished my document in no time, feeling really proud of myself and my still functioning brain with no sign of amnesia, made copies of it and sent it to all my kids, who marveled at their dad's exploit and experiences, and really appreciated our humble stock. Then they suddenly said that I should write my book in English so that all the grandkids and the upcoming generation could read and comprehend and appreciate their roots while acting and thinking as real Americans.

And that is why I had to spend some more times writing this book. Although roughly its content is the same covering my childhood in a middle class environment and my adulthood in an ever changing political scenery

with the trickiness, deceits, face saving concerns and the complicated ways of thinking and behaving of the Orientals which have been difficult to decipher using the normal American logical thinking. Then the tragic period of the demise of free Vietnam ending with the mass exodus to freedom with all means thinkable for all those that a blindfolded fate had selected.

According to the famous Book of Change of Confucean thinking, "when it is stuck there is change and change leads to freedom", and it was my good fate leading me to the last C-130 USAF flight out of Saigon to Guam the night of the 27th of April 1975. In America I had to show leadership for a family which for long had been used to an easy life and though it had not been an easy task the end result was a big success owing to hard work, determination and the ardent desire to emerge in a society of freedom, equality and under the rule of law.

Although it is not in my intention to show my opinion on the reason of the fast collapse of free Vietnam, but my recollection of some of the events in which I had been involved either as a living witness or as a team player would shed light on the very recent history of Vietnam prior to its quick demise like a castle built with a deck of playing cards.

PREFACE

What you are about to read---if I understand the author's plan---is deserving of a much wider audience. His family and friends will appreciate the drama and undoubtedly will be moved by it. Every American, native or immigrant, will laud his courage and his ability to find a bit of humor in tense situations.

Bob Tran's friends on the Monterey Peninsula have long admired his involvement in charitable works. Those who have not stood close to him may be astounded at the exciting twists and turns his life took in Vietnam.

This little book might well be made required reading for the children of those who came here following the fall of Vietnam. They stand on the shoulders of men like Bob Tran. Men who can take a licking and keep on ticking.

McNeill Archibald Gardner

CHAPTER ONE

I.-An uneventful youth

I was born in a family of teachers. My father taught school after graduating from Hue National College of Pedagogy, My mother was a preschool teacher in ThanhHoa. They met at the home of her older brother Do-vuong Tuong, who tutored him. My grandparents were wood turners in Nhi-Khe of the district of Thuong-Tin, Province of Ha-Dong, North Vietnam. In 1896 they gave birth to their youngest son, Tran-huu-Luong nicknamed Son after already having three much older ones Tran-quy-Quynh, Tran-ngoc-Ho and Tran-ngoc-Giao.

In 1897 there was a catastrophic flood and the people was subjected to famine and misery. They had to flee South looking for a better living. My father was only one year old and my grandma had to hand carry him all the way through strange places, crossing the Dong-Giao pass which had the reputation of fierce tigers and frightful spirits. My three uncles, being much older, were able to follow them, the sad sight of a ragtag group in search of food away from their native place. My grandpa had to hand carry all his wood turning tools.

After reaching Thanh Hoa, "land of limpid water and white rice" they camped out and opened their wood turning shed which became prosperous. The three older kids were sent to school but the youngest one being a spoiled baby stayed home shooting marbles and kicking balls with other kids and went to school only when he was fifteen. Being very intelligent he caught up very fast specially owing to the help of Mr. Tuong.

My maternal grand parents also emigrated from Nam-Dinh and were artisans of votive things and paper lanterns. They died relatively young and their two young daughters Minh and Nguyet had to live with brother Tuong who then worked at the custom service as assistant to the French boss in their hunt for bootleggers.

My father liked Miss Nguyet who then was considered the most beautiful woman of Thanh-Hoa and he asked for her hand right after graduation. My dad was a tall sportsman and during his school years in Hue he had become the captain of the soccer team there. At one time with a few Nghe-Tinh and Rhade friends he walked home four or five hundred kilometers afar through such places so hot and arid that he got blisters on his feet. But he said he could learn more of the country and know, for example, where the swamp of the Ho dynasty or the lagoon of Tam-Giang are. Besides, it was a saving of fee for transportation by the Pham-van-Phi bus. But from then on he would not dare anymore to repeat the same hardship.

After their wedding dad was assigned to the school of Phu-Dien in Nghe-An province and mom followed him. The place had the reputation of being a malaria infested country with the very virulent falsiparium bacteria and I contracted it when I was a very young kid.

Being a small frame person when she gave birth to me mom had to labor from noon the previous day until 3 a.m. the next day and when I was delivered the doctor said the boy failed and was dirt grey. Then one minute later he shouted in excitement that may be he can be saved hearing a very faint noise. Lifting me by holding up my ankles he gave a couple of raps to my back and the first cry was heard. My parents cherished their first baby so much that when I was one year old they took a photo of me sitting on the dining table while they sat on both sides and proudly showed to every one that here is our champagne bottle.

Because of my malaria disease I had many life and death situations. Finally a French doctor said there is a very dangerous way to cure the malady: an intravenous injection of quinine, but it could give a fatal shock. “If you want to give it a try both of you must sign a consent”. In a situation of complete despair my parents signed the paper and I was saved. I was born on the 28th of March 1922 or according to the lunar calendar the first day of the third month of the year of the dog. It was believed that a boy born on the first day of the month or a girl born on the fifteenth would have very good luck in life. But as I bear the sign of the dog I’d do nothing but running back and forth all day, nevertheless I’d be a faithful and dependable guy.

A Chinese fortune teller predicted that having the stars of “a horse followed by a tobacco pipe carrier” I’d have many travels for business. My parents nicknamed me “cu Nghe” meaning the little boy from Nghe-An but it could be translated into “the saffron boy” due to my green yellow complexion of a malaria sickened boy whose red cells were devoured by the disease.

After a while my father was transferred to the Vinh school as a ninth grade teacher. When I was three years old I knew all the letters of the alphabet and even started to spell and read being taught by my father using a stick to write on the sand. I used to follow dad to school sitting at the bottom pupil desk with Nguyen-quang-Trinh who was my dad’s preferred student and who became later minister of education. Trinh's older brother had been also an outstanding student of my father and I remember that at every Tet holiday their father took them to our place with trays of Xa-Doai oranges as presents and had the kids down on their knees bowing to dad as a sign of gratitude according to the old Confucean tradition. In the mean time my mother gave birth to three more siblings one each year. Next to me was Bach-Lien so named because she saw in a dream Quan In handing her a white lotus flower. Then came Kiem and Nhuong whose names were taken from the writing of Confucius.

I remember at that time school kids of all ages left their classes, dressed in all white garb and demonstrated their mourn for the patriot Phan-Chu-Trinh. The French secret service agents ran back and forth in full alert. Also teachers were secretely passing out among themselves the outlawed paper Le Paria of Nguyen-ai-Quoc. That is why my father's name was blacklisted and he was transferred to the school of district Nghi-Loc, seven kilometers south of Vinh. Though he became headmaster it was not a promotion because the school taught only up to seventh grade. And as Nghi-Loc was at the center of Soviet Nghe-Tinh it was a trap by secret services to monitor and check on him.

All four of us used to play in the school yard facing the highway and every day we saw them carting away corpses of those being executed, arms and legs dangling. Then came the terrible killing of Ton-that-Uy district chief of Nghi-Loc. That day he went out with his assistant and six militiamen in an inspection tour. They were ambushed by the communist insurgents, assassinated, cut into pieces and dumped in the sea.

His replacement Tran-mau-Trinh being a former NCO of the French army with the reputation of a cold blooded killer asked for the assignment of a French Legionaire squadron which then set up a machine gun to protect the district seat. (Mr. Uy is the father and father-in-law of my classmates Ton-that-Uan and Ha-thuc-Ky).

The atmosphere was very tense. To relax my father with the help of the teachers and the school warden proceeded to build a clay tennis court. On weekends they all went out to play and mother also tried her hand at the racket, dressed in white shorts, a really amazing sight at that time. My father was a very good tennis player. I remembered when the French champion Henry Cochet came to Vinh giving an exhibition match with Chim-Giao he took me with him to watch it.

When I was nine and in seventh grade Emperor Bao-Dai came for an inspection tour. All students were instructed to get down on their knees with faces looking down at the floor. I managed to take a quick glance at the king and saw a fair skin tall man dressed in gold color dress with a dragon embroidered at the front, wearing a gold color headdress and slowly walking with majesty. Wow, how can a man be so elegant and handsome!

When I had completed my seventh grade my mother took me to Vinh to go on with the next grade. She had me staying with the assistant teacher Mr Vinh's home. She bought for me a suitcase made of light brown wood and did not forget to put in a handful of bronze cent pieces. But it was my first time to be away from the family and I could not refrain from crying every day. Then one day in the school yard a rogue student threw a banana peel in my face, I could not stand it any longer and mom had to take me home. During that year I stayed home and I accompanied her to Ha-Tinh when she had to take my six month old little brother Loc with very high fever swathed in a thick blanket to be treated for pneumonia by Dr, Dang-van-Du.

In 1932 when Loc was one year old the whole family took the train to ThanhHoa for Tet. The night before Loc slept with my parents while the four of us slept together in a close by bed under mosquito net. The whole room had a small kerosene lantern giving a weak yellow light. While everyone was asleep I suddenly heard my father talking French to my mother, asking her to take an airplane flight with him. Being curious I looked out and saw on the mosquito net the shadow of dad stooping, "the sunlight caressing the camellia flower".

In ThanhHoa it was all fun being entertained by our uncles and auntie Chuong, who is the little sister of my father. My grandma always got me to sit next to her and help preparing her betel chew. Uncle and auntie Chuong also had a wood turning lathe from which they made candle holders, incense bowls and toys for kids. They also helped me up to their lathe but I was too short and my feet could not reach the pedals. They also fabricated wooden clogs, using a special ax to split jack fruit wood into square shaped pieces and then carved them cleverly into clogs which they polished with a curved plane.

My grandma is a big lady with a strong voice which permitted her to direct and manage the whole family after my grandpa died of alcoholism. All my three uncles finished ninth grade and worked for the railroad service as train controllers and for the hospital as head nurse. My oldest uncle had two children the handsome and tall Mr. Chau, who died by a disease puffing up his body which exuded a yellow liquid and the beautiful and slender miss Bao.

Once His Majesty Bao-Dai came to visit the city trade fair. All the beautiful girls of ThanhHoa had their heart throbbing wishing to catch the royal eyes and maybe, someone would go living in the royal palace. Miss Bao with her two friends had a show stand at the fair and she had the privilege to kneel down in front of the King to offer him a golden brocade scarf. Bao was later married to Prince Vinh-Pho who was the governor of Trieu-Tuong. the sanctified area of the Nguyen Dynasty.

Uncle Ho, having no children, had an affair with a neighbor woman and gave her a baby girl named Ty he brought home to raise. Ty was married to court clerk Cong in Phan-Thiet but after he died of tuberculosis she remarried to Ton-quang-Phiet a high ranking man of the Viet-Minh. In 1988 I received a letter from her urging me to go home and help the country saying that a certain Nguyen-tien-Hung formerly advisor to Nguyen-van-Thieu and knowing me gave that suggestion. I did not reply to her letter. As my aunt Mrs. Ho could not bear any children she had got her own young sister in to become my uncle's concubine but the end results were a string of girlies Nhi, An and Ai and still no boy.

In 1934 my parents gave birth to another boy Tran-do-Cam 12 years younger than I. Maybe they had felt tired of the whole thing and did not anymore go through the painstaking work of consulting the old book of Confucius to look for good words to name the boys. Instead, they used the locality names for that purpose. Loc and Cam came from district Nghi LOC and village Kim CAM. In 1935 dad was transferred to the school of Hoang-Hoa of the native Thanh-Hoa province and gave two more siblings named Hoang and Hoa, also every other year.

We were then only 14 km from the city of Thanh-Hoa. Then we could often pay visit to our grandma and the whole group. I was then in 9th grade and had to go to the city for my final exam. As students from all districts were there it was such a huge crowd that they had to erect sheds on the school yard. I graduated with high honors and received prizes from the King and the French Governor Pasquier, stacks of beautiful books leather bound and gilded titles. I stayed with uncle Tuong during the examination time and across from his place was the house of district chief Kieu from where two girls Khieu-thi-Khanh-Quy and Pham-thi-Phu-Xuan always poked their faces out for a quick glance at "such a young gifted man".

If my father was reassigned to a much better place it was owing to my mother dealing with Mr. Ta Hoan who is the father of her best friend Mrs. Tham Cao. Mr. Ta Hoan was then assistant to the secretary of education Pham-Quynh. Now mom could frequently board the trains south to Quang-Ngai to buy dried areca nuts and raw sugar for resale to the merchants of Thanh-Hoa among them I still remembered a blind old lady who is the mother of Dr. Nguyen-trinh-Co and my classmate Nguyen-trinh-Tiep.

We had also set up bins to store rice repaid by farmers after the harvest. My mother had given "loan of future rice" to be repaid in kind then. Lien and I always took turns counting and checking the many buckets of rice using memory bamboo sticks. Having saved some money my parents bought an old house in the city in 1937 at 40 Hospital Street and started to demolish it for building in place a brand new and spacious villa. Mom also bought a beautiful rickshaw with gilded metal accessories and trims. From time to time the four of us went with mom to visit uncle Tuong. The rickshaw was fully loaded and pulled by our driver, a strong muscled man, huffing, puffing and sweating through the 14 km stretch. It was really a feudal sight, human horse slaving to serve the bourgeoisie!

At home we had all kinds of servants, a female cook, a maid for my young brothers, a young girl to run errands and the rickshaw driver who also had to pound pork pate and thrash rice.

Life was comfortable and during one of her business trips southward my mom had a stopover in Hue begging Mr. Ta Hoan to clear my father's file. That is why dad had been reassigned to be school master of Dong-Son and ready to be promoted to school inspector. He also got the title of "Special Learner" and could wear the ivory plaque of the mandarins. Now during special holidays he worn black sheer tunique, head dressed with a black turban, wearing black shiny leather slippers and we could see on his puffed up breast a small proud mandarin white ivory plaque. Pa often said "wise girl makes the grade for the husband".

Our new house was built one half meter above ground and they filled the space under the floor with golden sand for insulation from ground humidity. From the street in one had to cross a wrought iron gate into a landscaped rose garden. On the left was the garage. Up the three step staircase was the front verandah before entering a spacious living room furnished with a long antiques display chest and a set of five armchairs surrounding an octagonal coffee table, all custom made, hand carved "gu" hardwood encrusted with mother of pearl designs. My mother had hired a team of craftsmen from Nam-Dinh who stayed in the home and finished the art works in three months. On the two sides of the chest were hung two long black lacquered plaques with gilded carved Chinese characters of two verses written by an old poet of ancient studies which said:

"In the books tower Spring is in full bloom and mother is warm",

"On the mandarinal ocean the fresh breeze blows thru the citadels of oysters and cranes".

Fresh breeze are the names of the parents-in-law and citadels of oysters and cranes depicted the provinces of Nghe-An and Thanh-Hoa.

On the left hand side was my father's study looking out to the rose garden and on the other side is their bedroom. Just behind the living room was the dining room with a table made of maple wood and eight chairs, sandwiched between two smaller bedrooms.

Stepping out to the rear verandah we could look down to a garden planted with fruit trees surrounding a water well. The big boys used to bathe around the well, pulling up buckets of sweet and limpid water and dousing each other noisily.

On the left hand side of the house was a wide alley way paved with red clay bricks from Bat-Trang with four green slender areca palm trees in planters. This is where we used to play marbles and kick shuttlecocks. I remember when tap dancing was in vogue we also had steel plates nailed to our clogs and practiced dancing all day long until one day when father was tired of having his siesta disturbed, got us inside, had us lie belly down bare butts and gave each one of us five painful rattan sticks whips.

Behind the house, surrounding the vast garden was a series of brick constructions in L shape. Along the left were two study rooms for us, at the corner was the restroom and along the back wall adjacent to the neighbor property was a long brick shed housing the kitchen and the rice thrashing equipment. We often played in this area and it was here that I witnessed ma's mood changing from normally mellow and sweet to steely cold and very severe face the next time around. During summer vacation from Hue I used to come down here and tinker with cooking in the kitchen. I remember one day, I had seen people cook soybean soup in Hue and I bought some soybeans, processed them into fine mush and cooked soybean soup for the whole family.

In 1943, after a five year break my mother gave birth to the last male offspring Tran-do-Thien so named because my dad had then become president of the Thanh-Hoa Buddhist association. Again they were not anymore overexcited and they had procrastinated, registering for his birth certificate only in 1945.

Sister Lien had become the purser for the family, specially when mom traveled in business or when she was busy tending to her tontine affairs. Lien was the only rich one among us. I remembered when a family from Hue came to open an ice cream shop in town Lien gave Loc a nickel to buy a mung bean stick. Loc being only six then. wearing a light brown shirt with a dark brown short, raced up town in earnest to do it. On the return leg he had to lick the drops of melted ice cream and the stick had become skinnier. When Lien started to cut it into portions for us Kiem said that as Loc had already enjoyed the melted cream he won't get any share, to that Loc burst into heartbreaking tears and he finally was given his fair portion.

During her spare time Lien used to write poems under the pen name Lina and had them published in the Women Magazine. Teenage boys just milled around and they nicknamed her "Lien the clarinet" because she'd smile from ear to ear with everyone. Among them was Thuat, the son of Mr. Ca Ban and one of my father's pupils. Mother did not like him. But the boy was smart always hiding behind bushes awaiting for mom to go out to come in and flirt with Lien.

I went to college after my graduation. The school being about a block from home every morning we saw all the professors passing by with a stack of books on their arms. The Director was Mr. Thai-nguyen-Dao, a mix blood looking man (grandfather of songstress Thanh-Lan). I had outstanding grades being always at the top tiers for French, and for chemistry and physics as well as history and geography I never failed my A.

We loved so much swimming that along with my brothers Kiem and Nhuong we always went to the irrigation canal for a dip dawn to dark, swimming and diving to our heart content. We had become so tanned that friends called me Cung-the-black and Kiem was given the nickname of Bozambo. Every first day of Tet we always took a plunge in the icy cold water of the irrigation reservoir for luck and got out of there shivering and white.

We also practiced martial arts under the training of the son of Thanh-Hoa postmaster. At one time I went out with a city youth gang armed with bat and steel knuckles to "punish the Indian shopkeepers up street". I remembered when the movie theater of Mr. Hoang-van-Ngoc gave away beautiful movies "plaquettes" I saved a bountiful collection of those memorabilia.

Then came the fad of having hairdos Robert Taylor style. Every boy would buy hair cream and comb his forehead lock into oxen like horn. Came the time when each and everyone liked wearing "Flechet" hats as seen in movies. I wanted so much to have one and mom had to go to Tan-thanh-Vinh to buy it. It was a cream color hat displaying a thick sheep fur like nap, decidedly much better looking than the brownish ones of others.

Tan-thanh-Vinh was a specialty shop selling all kinds of imported French foods like ham, sausage and candies and pastries. Every time she went there she would buy those mouth watering sweets for us to enjoy. I still remember those round cans of "pastilles Valda" and the square red boxes of Sunmaid raisins. The manager of Tan-thanh-Vinh is the brother of Mr. Lam-Cat who is Cam's father-in-law.

Every boy knew by heart the love songs of Tino Rossi and Rina Ketty and they always whistled the tune Rose Marie by Nelson Eddy and Jeannette McDonald. The governor of Thanh-Hoa, H.E. Nguyen-Hy had two beautiful daughters Ngoc-Tram and Ngoc-Nhuy who went to the catholic Sisters School in a shiny black limo driven by a chauffeur wearing a red conical hat. We always looked at them in awe and admiration but it was a big surprise when Ngoc-Tram became my classmate in Hue Khai-Dinh Lycee and afterwards was a stunning songstress famous for her rendition of Blue Danube and "the withering night of Ben-Ngu" by Duong-thieu-Tuoc.

Our house sat across from the city hospital and the residence of Dr. Chesneau. After turning right and going for about 500 meters one would come to the old Vauban wall surrounded by a perimeter moat planted with lotus. The moat had plenty of shrimp and we used to fish them and take back to our cook to have good soup made. We used chicken intestine as bait and the shrimp were big eaters. Each of us tended four or five bamboo rods in the same time and when we pulled them out shrimp would cling to the bait shaking their tails.

By going along the moat for a short distance we'd reach Left Gate street and the house of uncle Co-Ky, my mom's oldest brother having a watch repair shop. Uncle Co-Ky graduated from the poly technical school and was an expert in motors and steel works. He had a fair rose color skin just like uncle Tuong, a very distinct feature of the Do family unlike our tanned complexion and I always was kidding saying that we were descendants of Tran-thu-Do the fisherman.

Speaking of our origin, having lost all family record books after so many changes and upheavals, the only thing we knew then is that when my grandparents fled the flood and then my grandpa died prematurely due to alcohol we did not know him. One time brother Cam went home, trying to look for traces of our roots discovered that we belonged to the Tran-Dinh family and there still is a family temple in Nhi-Khe which would be opened only once a year. Well, the only sure thing we know now is that when the family reached Thanh-Hoa we were dirt poor and food hungry. To say that our forefather name must have been "Tran-nhu-Nhong", or "bare like a worm" is not too far from the truth.

Time flew, I had completed my four years of college and got my "diplome" certificate DEPSI. I had to go to Hue for an admission test to Lycee Khai-Dinh. Mom accompanied me to the Capital City by a night train stopping every now and then for more passengers and we arrived very early the next morning. Mom checked in at Hotel de la Gare and we took a rickshaw ride to the examination school the next day. I felt completely lost and shy and wondered how I could manage if mom was not there. Only now I can realize how sharp and fast my mother was.

There were so many candidates from the colleges of Vinh, Qui-Nhon and the Hue private schools of Providence,

Pellerin and Thuan-Hoa competing for only forty slots. I was lucky to get it, mom was so proud and she took me to a restaurant in Ben-Ngu for a bowl of beef noodle and the famous Hue pancake.

Back home, I enjoyed my remaining summer break and walked the 14 km stretch to the seaside resort of Samson with a couple of friends. I was hosted by a fisherman family and was treated to excellent fares of fresh caught sea foods. Each day I went to the white sand beach swimming or going along it commingling with groups of youth from Hanoi playing guitars and singing the most up to date love songs. I remembered specially the young lads of the very rich Mrs. Hoa-Tuong Dang-Ky and Dang-Co dressed in Hawaian shirts around the beautiful Alice Trang singing O Sole Mio of Tino Rossi. I also went up hill to admire the elegant resort villas of the French and specially the one belonging to Francois Maurice Giao also known as Phan-van-Giao owner of a big Pharmacy in Thanh-Hoa and the future governor of central Viet-Nam.

Summer vacation drew to a close and I had to be ready to proceed to the Capital City for school. Mom had bought for me a big trunk with brass trim to secure all my things and my parents sent me off at the city railway station. But when the train started rolling out, their sight receded while their son's mind looked forward to a new horizon of hope and promises.

The train compartment was tight with all kinds of female merchants noisily talking and spitting betel chew to the floor as if there were no one around. When we reached Vinh there was a group of young men climbing up. They looked like students of Nghe-An going to Hue, rough looking guys, dressed with off color white garbs and with a black umbrella hooked to the shoulder, completely odd comparatively to the spit polished boys from Thanh-Hoa. The train had a short stop at Lang-Co and food vendors ran along offering all kinds of delicacies among them the steamy hot and flavorful fish soup.

The train arrived at Hue in the wee hours but there were already a group of rickshaws awaiting to take you to the school. The huge entry portal was barred with a concrete screen and the rickshaws were not permitted to drive through. We all had to haul as we could our trunks through and meet the supervisors who guided us upstairs to our beds and lockers. When all our belongings were neatly arranged and secured in the lockers we had to put the trunks in an indicated corner for the school warden to take to storage.

That evening during the first dinner a big fight occurred between the Nghe's and the Quang's just because they mock at each other's funny accent. There is that old saying "to insult one's father is milder than to mock one's accent" and it perfectly fit the situation. I was not able to take a single bite since all dishes were so spicy displaying a visible sheen of peppery hot stuff. Nevertheless I saw some guys taking out of their pocket a big green pepper to chew with pleasure as dessert.

The schedule for us boarders was very strict and tight. At six in the morning the supervisor on duty woke us up to remake our bed and do our morning cleanup chores. Then we had to go downstairs to the classroom for our homework. At precisely eight o'clock we all had to be in line in the corridor with others students and orderly entered the classrooms.

I sat at the left front row right across from the huge blackboard covering the whole wall. On the right side sat the seven girls, five Vietnamese Nguyen-thi-Ngoc-Tram,

Le-thi-Ngoc-Anh, Nguyen-thi-Bach-Hac, Ton-nu-Nhu-Mai and Tran-thi-Tung and two French girls, Madeleine Cozic and Celine Loisy.

The atmosphere was essentially austere, the silence only disturbed by the screeching of chalk on the blackboard and the even tone of the professors' voice. Boys wore long black tunics over white trousers and had wooden clogs. Only three among us displayed western pants and white short sleeve shirts. They were Hoang-kim-Nha, Tran-van-Dinh and Nguyen-chau-Phung sitting behind the misses.

The professors were all French educated and in the range of more or less thirty years of age: Professor Nguyen-duong-Don, a handsome and mild mannered man, married to a German lady teaching algebra; professor Nguyen-thuc-Hao a tiny man teaching geometry nicknamed pocket teacher and always drawing perfect circles on the blackboard; professor Nguyen-huy-Bao as tall as a French man teaching philosophy and always reminding us that "God is all powerful and compassionate"; professor Pham-dinh-Ai with a very strong voice, forehead balding, teaching physics and chemistry and who became later senator but being fed up with things was seen sitting on the sidewalk of Saigon rumbling and mumbling; professor Ung-Qua, widower, teaching literature and during the sessions of Vietnamese dissertation of Kieu famous poetry had even played the citar making Ngoc-Tram's heart racing; the talented arts teacher, rotund professor Ton-that-Dao; Father Gagne, Canadian, English teacher whose face changed to completely red when talking to the girls and the youngest of them, professor Nguyen-thieu-Lau of geography always wondering about the formation of the lagoon of Cau-Hai.

The afternoon class ended at five and we had a short break before going for dinner at six and on again to the classroom for doing homework under supervision until nine, which was bed time. Our beds were clean at first because during summer break the school had them fully sanitized and debugged. But later on some of the bugs eggs hatched and soon there was an infestation of them crawling about and biting us at night.

A few months later one of our friends named Do-duc-Duc was drowned on the Perfume River and the whole class went to his burial. When he was buried the girls burnst into sobbing tears and everyone cried showing that when you are young you may be easily moved and overwhelmed with emotion.

Then came the shocking news of Ngoc-Tram being married to professor Ung-Qua. It was heard that her family was not pleased because of a twenty years gap between them. Besides her grandma is also direct descendant of the royal family like Mr. Ung-Qua and it was a no-no for same blood marriage. We were told that Tram made a family revolt, bringing out a straw mat and kneeling down in front of grandma, bowed her head to the floor asking for forgiveness because she had decided to move on with her life and love. The news spread like wild fire among the classmates who were very unhappy with the romantic teacher. Sometimes later it was learned that Tram had left her lover and one of our friends during a Tet visit to Mr. Ung-Qua had asked him about her to that he gave a still very romantic answer "the red lacquered cage is still open, the bird flies out free and it will feel free to return".

At the end of that year the Imperial Court celebrated the 10th birthday of Prince Bao-Long. The ceremony was at the huge auditorium of Providence school of the Redemptorist fathers. A stage was set up high over the floor on which sat His Majesty Bao-Dai and Empress Nam-Phuong dressed in full ceremonial garbs. Prince Bao-Long also dressed in a bright golden royal uniform sat between them. Lycee Khai-Dinh selected a number of students of uniform size to be paired with school girls of Dong-Khanh wearing blue tunics and head dressed in gold color crown to march in and offer bouquets of flowers to the royal prince. I was chosen to be with Miss Pham-thi-Hoan the youngest daughter of Prime Minister Pham-Quynh.

In the royal palace compound there were also all kinds of ceremonial activities witnessed by the royal family sitting high up over the Ngo-Mon gate. Students of all schools orderly proceeded through in front of them waving small gold color flags and shouting Hoang-De-Van-Tue (Long Life to the Emperor). But the very unruly kids mockingly shouted Hoang-De-Dai-Me, which sounded similar but meaning “Be the Emperor wetting his bed”.

The two years of study were almost over and we had to be fully ready to pass the examination for the certificate of “baccalaureat one” with a team of examiners coming from other places. We worried with the coming of professor Pham-Duy-Khiem having the high degree of doctor of grammar from Paris. He had the reputation of a very strict, meticulous and difficult person to grade your French essay and if you did not pass with a minimum B you would fail the whole affair. I succeeded and got my degree with a high color A.

Back to Thanh-Hoa with the family mom had already busily begun to search for the appropriate mate for me. She considered the girls of the Do’s family in the district of Tho-Hac but she said “those maids were not appropriate because they seemed lazy and doing nothing all along except enjoying an easy life”. Finally she seemed eager to focus her eyes at Miss Thu, the only child of the rich owner of the chinese traditional pharmacy Thang-Long, and always seen busy working in the store. But I said that she was chubby and as short as a jack fruit nut and besides with a still very much idealistic mind I would not like having the reputation of a "gold digger type".

And then the whole thing was quickly forgotten and the end of summer vacation came and I had to be prepared to go back to Hue for my last year and my degree of baccalaureat of mathematics. We had only boys in the math class, all girls preferred the philosophy study. There were not many of them left since some got married while others quit to become teachers. The math curriculum was very heavy and complex but for me it was not too difficult. Nevertheless I failed my first session because I was too preoccupied pursuing the dream of going to Japan for further study trying to work it out through the connection of my classmate Tran-van-Dinh who sometimes later became the information secretary in the government of Ngo-dinh-Diem.

My grand mother Nguyen-thi-Vy, the grand lady leader of the whole clan (circa 1936)

My parents circa 1965

CHAPTER TWO

II.- A Period of Upheaval

As said above I was getting prepared for the math degree in 1942. In the dormitory everyone was so eager to review all the subject matters that all night long we all gathered in the corner close to the restroom, squatting or lying on the tile floor, books and documents scattered all around, bare torsos wet of perspiration studying in spite of the attacks from mosquitoes or bugs.

Then on mid-Spring of that year one special event distracted and preoccupied me so much that I lost my interest and failed the first exam. I only succeeded in the second session to be awarded the degree of bachelor of mathematics and go on to the university of Hanoi and enroll in the classes of special mathematics at the Albert Sarraut Lycee and General Mathematics of the faculty of sciences.

Back to that mid-spring time of 1942, the Imperial Japanese Army gradually turned up the screws on the French administration. One of my classmates, Tran-van-Dinh asked me and two others Vo-quang-Ho and Nguyen-trinh-Tiep, to join him in his native village of Truoi to discuss the possibility of going to Japan for higher study. At his home we saw that Dinh had a Japanese army jockey hat and even displayed a long shiny Japanese sword. We were secretly introduced to the Japanese Consulate General in Hue.

One very stormy rainy day we discreetly went out to the place disguised with a conical hat and dressed in a palm leaves raingear to have our Japanese passports made, ready to board a ship to Tokyo after the first group of the misses Ly and Dao, Dr. Dang-van-Ngu and Mr. Nguyen-thanh-Nguyen. But then the war in the Pacific intensified and there were no ships in sight and I was so distracted by the event that I failed my first session of the examination.

I went to the Sciences Faculty of Hanoi in a very ardent frame of mind full of idealism and the desire to serve the country. There I had the opportunity to rub off with the famous names of the three areas of Vietnam. The official name of the Hanoi University was French University of Indochina serving not only Tonkin, Annam and Cochinchina but also the two neighboring countries of Laos and Cambodia. Therefore the atmosphere was for broadmindedness and freedom.

The French Decoux Administration strived earnestly to gain the hearts of students and built a complete campus called Cite Universitaire of Indochina, a very modern complex with all the amenities. I was admitted in building B which was the newly completed second home with six apartments having eight individual studios each.

The buildings had three floors, each with two apartments and the ground floor was a big hall furnished with comfortably luxurious leather arm chairs and hardwood coffee tables, and in one corner was a piano. Among the students quartered in apartments there were tutors in individual separate studios on both sides of the top floor. Tutors were advanced students designated often among those in their fourth year of medical school.

Among tutors I still remember Huynh-van-Huon, Pham-phu-Khai, Nguyen-danh-Dan, Phan-thanh-Hoa and Pham-thanh-Vinh. The basement was where you hung your bicycles up. And the students dining facility was also there serving two menus, French and local as paid and desired by the students.

From the building out was a spacious and well groomed space showing on the left hand side basket ball, volley ball courts and an old pagoda which was converted into a small restaurant offering a menu of Southern fares of pork skin noodles and Saigon pancakes under the management of Mrs Sau and Mrs Ba.

By following a paved wide alley out you reached the Bach-Mai street, a dusty and full of potholes thoroughfare going down town. There was also a tramway track leading to the Hoan-Kiem lake and some very daring and hardy students used to jump in and out on their way to the University at Bobillot avenue.

As for me and the majority of us, we biked all the way each and every day to school. Those from the South riding their shiny dura bike and as for us from Central and Northern areas we were pleased with our older means having mostly no brake and bell and wearing half-buttoned shirts looking like a group of hard hardened guys. In apartment six I was with seven other room mates, Vu-tam-Hoan, Tran-van-Bao, Nguyen-tan-Hong, Dang-quoc-Quan, Nguyen-duc-Quamg, Truong-xuan-Dan and Tze-shan-Nam. Quan and I were the only two in Sciences studies, all others did medical school, noisily and bluntly talking, and after their class in dead body dissection they showed excitement by drawing the vagina on the door with chalk.

Every morning I rode my bike to Bobillot avenue and while in class though listening intently to our professors we still had to chase away those enormous striped mosquitoes landing en force on our thighs and legs. After class I went to the library to do my home works and additional research. Back to the campus I normally would go out to play basketball with very good players like Hoang-xuan-Binh, Nguyen-trong-Thuong, Le-thieu-Huy, Nguyen-tan-Hong and so on. Life was very worriless and healthy.

From time to time there were special activities with AGEI (general association of students of Indochina) like the paintings exposition of Diep-minh-Chau and Nguyen-van Sang, the piano-violin chamber duet of Do-the-Phiet and Nguyen-trong-Thuong attracting a vast attendance of the elegant and the famous of the capital city.

Talking of AGEI each year there was an election for a new president. Duong-duc-Hien was the 1943 chairman presiding over a board of representatives from various faculties: Nguyen-nhu-Kim for Sciences, Nguyen-tu-Vinh for Medical school and for Law school there were those famous orators like Phan-My. In Spring of each year there was a students festival show at the Ha-Noi Opera complete with speeches, songs, music and dramas. That year I performed the horsey dance with eleven other students dressed in all white suits under the direction of Phan-thanh-Hoa. Hoa also conducted the student choir singing "The March of The Students".

On December 1944 they organized a cross country race starting from building A with about 200 participants. The event began at 6 of a very cold misty morning. We ran through thick grass muddy fields, swam across a canal on a 20 km circuit and many dropped out midway. I was the first one at the arrival followed by fifty others with a few French students among the pack.

Every weekend the association organized excursions on bikes to several spots so that we could know more of the country, furthering our sense of patriotism, One time we visited the Chua-Huong temple and while climbing the numerous steep steps winding up the mountain to the temple we all sang patriotic songs with combative lyrics.

Another time we visited the vestiges of the Ly dynasty and inspected the hundred-door pagoda of Bac-Ninh. During the Tet holidays of that year a group of hardy guys participated in a lengthy biking trip up the mountains for a pilgrimage to the tomb of the national hero King Le-Loi and winding down to Trieu-Tuong paying respect to the tomb of Nguyen-Kim founder of the Nguyen dynasty.

With encouragements from friends I joined the rover boy scouts group Lam-Son of chief Hoang-dao-Thuy nick name Ho-Sut or broken tooth tiger. My section under the leadership of Dr. Pham-bieu-Tam had Hoang-kim-Hai, Nguyen-Ken, Nguyen-nhu-Kim, Nguyen-van-Chien, Pham-Quy, Le-ba-Hoan, Nguyen-trinh-Tiep, Ton-that-Hoang, Dang-van-Viet, big names during the war against the French. After a period of challenges I was bestowed a scarf to be given to me by chief Ho-Sut at a campground in Lang that night. A few members were supposed to go along with me but as no one showed up I understood that it was another trial for me. Then in the mid of a very dark and thick night I ventured out probing the route by myself and finally arriving on time at the spot where a big camp fire was ongoing and members were throwing in logs swearing to be faithful and to serve the country. When chief Ho-Sut wrapped the scarf on my shoulders I was so moved that tears ran down my cheeks.

During the summer break my section went camping at Ba-Vi. But the camping spot was not at altitude 400 meters which was the resort place. Instead of we moved upward to altitude 1,100 meters, an area having no soul except for trees in the jungle. We biked all the way from Hanoi to the base of the mountain and from there up we loaded our things, cooking utensils, blankets, foodstuff and rice on the bicycles frame and hiked up pushing the heavily loaded bicycles along to the summit. There we had to gather stones and arrange them as a temporary bed for the night. Nguyen-Ken, the student of forestry directed the felling of trees to build a log house.

I was in charge of cooking for the whole group and as we all worked very hard the supply of food dwindled quickly to nothing left. I went down to altitude 400 to buy rice and haul up on my bike. I also looked under stones and crevices to catch stone crabs for soup and went into the forest for those edible wild legumes for our need of survival during the week. At the end of the camping time we proceeded down hill and we had only one good night sleep on the log floor that was finished then. Back to Hanoi we had dinner at a restaurant on the Hoan-Kiem lake shore and one could see on the table all the empty Hommel beer bottles, each and every one of us having downed more than ten bowls of rice.

In 1944 Pham-thanh-Vinh, a law student, was elected president to replace the out going Duong-duc-Hien. He looked like an austere mandarin, always dressed in black satin robe just like a new district administrator. During that period the French secret services were very active. There was a rumor among us that Duong-duc-Hien had left town to join the guerilla zone and we all discreetly talked of the Viet-Minh. I passed with success the examination for the degree of General Mathematics and went on to study Rational Mechanics and Integral and differential Calculus.

Once in a while during important holidays break I rode my bike back home in Thanh-Hoa. The stretch was about 150 km passing by the towns of Phu-Ly and Ninh-Binh then crossing the Dong-Giao pass. But it had become a very daunting venture since all bridges were destroyed by bombs from US planes. One time I had to carry my bike on my shoulder crossing the dry bed of a river. Mid way my legs sank into muddy soil and it was with unthinkable efforts I had finally extracted my feet free but one boot got loose and stayed buried down in the muddy stuff. I pulled my dear bike to the other side of the river, lay down a good while to recover my strength and will and then I went back to find the spot to finally dig out the lost boot.

Another time I went back home for the wedding of Lien and Thuat. I accompanied the bride to Di-Linh about 40km North-West of Thanh-Hoa. Thuat's father Mr. Ca Ban settled up here after his dad emigrated in with all the poor people of his village to develop and set up this ranch. All of Thuat uncles also lived here, each one in a bungalow built on a green hilltop, using horses to move around. During my few days stay Thuat had trained me horse riding and both of us racing day in day out up and down the green hilly landscape exhilarated. I wore GI boots bought at the flea market was dressed with an old GI uniform and a red woolen knitted skull cap. I looked really odd and funny but I had the feeling to be in an American Far West movie.

Back to Hanoi I witnessed the big famine killing millions of people. Many villages in the delta of North Vietnam were completely wiped off the map. People old and young carrying their belongings and sometime the ancestors altars flocked out aimlessly in search of food and survival. All looked harrowed with eyes poking out and they devoured whatever they could get. Even the trees lining the streets of Hanoi had their bark gnawed off and black skinny cadavers were scattered every where, on sidewalks at gutters and in front of houses doors.

Every morning along with boy scout friends we went out with carts to gather corpses and take them like wood logs to a central place for trucks to haul to a mass burying dump in Giap-bat. One time I had witnessed a very heart breaking scene. When a Japanese military truck full of sacks of rice went through town stopped at an intersection it was assaulted by hordes of hungry and bony men trying to climb aboard. The soldiers fought them back with their gun butts and bayonets but the poor hungry kept on biting, clawing the sacks to eat mouthful of scattered raw rice.

Houses put kettles of bran soup out of their front door for the miserable lots and even at our campus mess we were served only plates of moldy and smelly noodles.

That year I biked back to ThanhHoa with the family. Along the way was seen all the dried out human bodies scattered both sides of the highway. One sight still appears vivid in my memory nowadays. After reaching the summit of the Dong-Giao and racing down hill I suddenly saw about 200 meters ahead of me the silhouette of a woman staggering along through the amber sunset light. When I reached the spot the woman suddenly collapsed and died still holding in her arms her infant sucking her tit. I pulled them aside of the roadway and went on my mind numb and my heart saddened.

In 1944 I got my certificate of rational mechanics. On 9 March of 45 the Japanese toppled the French at midnight. We all were very excited, removed the curtain rods to use as weapons and assembled in the mess hall. Passed midnight Bui-Diem came with Miss Anita Kim and Yamaguchi, a Japanese agriculture student. They informed us of the successful operation and gave us the advice to surround and incarcerate all French students. We were all overexcited and armed with sticks and whatever things we could get as weapons we went out to arrest them and secure them in the villa which was the office of Dr. Rivoalen pending their herding away by the Japanese authority. The next morning Colonel Kudo came meeting with us in the hall of building B and suggested to select a new board of directors. I did not know why the students present at that time elected me to replace Rivoalen, Le-van-Thuan to replace Lafont as secretary general and Pham-phu-Khai as purser. I went on to occupy the desk of Rivoalen but did not have a single notion of management and budget. I was chauffered in the shiny limo of Rivoalen displaying a flag of the national gold color. So with only 22 years of age and having no knowledge of administration I had the feeling of a blind man being led by a seeing eye dog. I wondered what kind of star was in my fortune teller's prediction? A few days later Professor Rivoalen came for a meeting with me. I treated him very courteously but he only asked very politely for the tri-color French flag which I gave back to him.

Came the Two Trung Sisters Holiday which was also designated as Vietnamese Women Day with meeting and entertainments at the Hanoi Opera House. I was invited as guest of honor. The very young Director was dressed in the only and one suit of white stripes light blue wool custom made at "The Silver Scissors" in Hue as a gift from mom after his graduation of Baccalaureat one.

When the limo with the golden flag fluttering came to a stop at the entrance to the opera house a female voice announced ceremoniously "the director's arrival" and all the beauties of Hanoi got busy around me leading me to the VIP booth. Among them I remembered were Miss Nhu of the To-Chau store and Miss Pham-le-Trinh daughter of the well known Pham-le-Bong and so many other misses around me pinning insignia on my lapel and speaking like birdies with musical and lovely voices. Then came the moment when they presented baskets seeking donations to the association. The young director had just a little money in his wallet and he had to scrape them off all out to put in the basket. Well, it was a near tragedy situation!

Then the students exhibit show, an annual event, was set up in the courtyard of the Hanoi mayor's building. It always was a very famous show attracting the whole Hanoi where the mothers or brothers of "full moon" daughters and sisters took them to, leisurely going back and forth looking for the potential young men within the frame of mind of "not university student no mate". Along with Pham-mau-Quan we set up our science booth bringing all and everything from the lab out for display.

While we were busy explaining to guests X-rays and cathodic rays the good friend Nguyen-tan-Hong wearing a "front line assault hat" just like myself dropped by with three young elegant misses dressed in light blue color gowns and introduced them to me "Vinh my fiancée and her two nieces". I nodded politely and went back to my job. Then we greeted Bui-Diem and his fiancée along with her two young sisters.

The official paper of AGEI was "The Monome" published in French. After March 9, 1945 it was changed to "Tu-Tri" (autonomy) written in Vietnamese as a tool of dissemination of revolutionary ideals of the General Federation of the Vietnamese Students. At one time I went with Le-van-Giang and Nguyen-Ken to Central Vietnam to distribute the papers. While we stopped over at Phu-Ly we stayed overnight at the home of Mr. Bui-Ky the father of Bui-Diem. The next morning before continuing our trip South we were given a box of sticky rice with chicken by Pham-xuan-Chieu.

Coming to Thanh-Hoa I stayed with the family while the others went on to Nghe-An with a big stack of papers. The publishing office was in the campus. I belonged to the editorial team with Nguyen-sy-Quoc, Pham-van-Hai, Nguyen-xuan-Sanh, Le-khanh-Can, etc. The articles gradually changed scopes, indirectly criticizing the Nippon Army with humoristic drawings making the Japanese very upset (our friend Pham-van-Hai was a real artist designing caricatures and carving them on wood blocks for printing). We did not go to school and spent all our time discussing on articles to be published and doing things that were unsuitable to the policy of the Japanese. After about three months Colonel Kudo came back and took the administration of the campus in his hands and expelled us out.

One good Samaritan lent us his villa facing the Thien-Cuong lake and we moved in. The campus kitchen still provided us food in secret. And we went on writing articles changing from the theme “autonomy” to “independence” showing a more virulent and combative wording. The name of the paper changed to “Gio Moi” (new wind). For a few months we were under extreme tension with the scrutiny and surveillance of the Japanese Kempetai.

In August an informant let us know that the Japanese was mounting a midnight operation against us. Then we disbanded in secret. Along with Nguyen-xuan-Sanh and Le-khanh-Can we biked to the village of Quynh-Loi seeking asylum in the villa of professor Hoang-xuan-Han. Professor Han was not home but Mrs Han agreed to shelter us in the pigs pen away from the house. We stayed in there for a few days during which we were supplied with meals brought about by a little girl.

Day after day until the 14th of August when we learned that the war was drawing to a close and that the Japanese morale became low we ventured out in the open and we rode our bicycles South. In Thanh-Hoa I stayed with the family while the two others went to SamSon. On the 16th when news came out about the drop of an atomic bomb on the Japanese soil we knew that the war was ending and the Viet Minh activities intensified.

That morning an old classmate drop by to see me telling me that there will be an uprising to seize power. He called me "comrade" and said "we were aware of your patriotic activities in Hanoi and the Viet-Minh would give you a special mission: To seize the district of Phu Quang on the 18th". I eagerly accepted the offer and he gave me a gold-star insignia along with a red flag with gold star, telling me to keep it well hidden and displaying out only when I arrived at the district seat gate. He gave me a liaison address and did not forget to say that there will be a company of revolutionary soldiers to back me up on site.

Early that morning I biked out in direction South West for about 30 km. I came to the spot, a thatched hut with three peasants, one of them swinging leisurely on a hammock while the other two were squatting near by smoking their water pipe or sipping green tea. When seeing me entering they gave me the direction to the district seat. They told me to display my insignia only at the gate and then hoist the Viet Minh flag up without forgetting to say that one company of armed revolutionary soldiers will be there to back me up when needed.

When I arrived at the gate the militia man on duty dropped his gun and ran away. I picked up the gun, went in, lowered the old flag and hoisted up the new one while all the people at the place ran away climbing the perimeter wall in panic. And I did not see a single revolutionary man at the ready there.

Afterwards thinking back of my exploit I realized the trick of the Viet Minh to use the ardent patriotism of the people to achieve their purpose. If at that moment that militia man fought back I would be the only dead man there! I also knew afterwards that the insignia and the flag were made by my sister.

The next day 19th of August was the general uprising day and the whole city population went out to the streets demonstrating under the direction of young men using loudspeakers. I was in charge of security marching along the sidewalk wearing a pistol with only one bullet. The crowd proceeded to the city soccer field shouting revolutionary slogans and hearing the exhortations of Mr. Huong Trac on revolutionary spirit.

Afterwards I worked for the security office under M. Trung a well known man of the city. We went out searching residences of the French and of those called pro French traitors. In the search of the villa of Mr. Ha-van-Vuong, the prominent son of a Muong dignitary named Ha-trieu-Nguyet we found ingots of silver as big as bricks but they disappeared completely after being brought back to the office. In my ten days there I witnessed a complete mess and corruption and I decided to quit and stay home, disappointed.

On 2nd September the news of Ho-chi-Minh declaration of independence and the hearing of the resignation of

Emperor Bao-Dai with his historical statement "to feel better as the citizen of a free country than the king of a subjugated one" my morale went up. And on the 4th of the month with all my belongings in my back pack I rode my bicycle back to the capital city.

When I reached Phu-Ly it rained so hard that I went into a beef soup joint waiting for the storm to run its course. Then I saw in there Dang-van-Sung with his two cousins Dang-van-But and Dang-van-Nghien on their way from Nghe-An with the same frame of mind hoping that the situation would be better than in the provinces. We all regained the campus, swollen hearts and disoriented spirits.

During that time the Chinese army under Generals Lu-Han and Tieu-Van came to accept the surrender of the Japanese. A number of Vietnamese expatriates of the Vietnam Quoc-Dan-Dang (Vietnam nationalist party) like Nguyen-hai-Than and Vu-hong-Khanh came back under their coattail.

In the streets vendors sold all kinds of GI stuffs, like sardines, spam, cheese cans and also US military blankets and gears to the enthusiastic reception of the general population. I bought some of those things and took back to our room to cook for all friends to enjoy with a pot of sticky rice.

Then occurred the Ngu-Xa event and everyday Phan-quang-Dan and others leading figures of the VNQDD took turn to broadcast harsh criticisms of the Viet-Minh and the communists. Some days I went out to Ngu-Xa with my close buddy Nguyen-tan-Hong bringing along sandwiches to sit down on the sidewalk and listen to those propaganda broadcasts.

On campus there were visits of high ranking names of the Viet-Minh like Tran-van-Giau who came to exhort the students to support the cause. And there were intense discussions on the name of the association to be changed to association of students for the safeguard of the country. An atmosphere of mistrust was present completely different from the unanimity inherent to us from the onset. I also went back to class like others but we were completely distracted with nerves worn raw.

During that time because of disrupted communications due to the bombardment by the Americans we mostly did not often receive money from our family. When we had some cash buddy Hong and I went to a small restaurant next to South Gate for a satisfying and appetizing meal of which I still remember now the flavor of the soup bowl of tomatoes with back ribs and eggs.

When we were cash poor we rode to street Lo-Su to eat at the tiny stall for rickshaw drivers serving a steaming hot rice with a plate of boiled legumes and a few pieces of pork meat having more fat than meat. I had to tutor mathematics for a few boys of rich families to supplement my meager income. At times I followed Hong to his fiancee's home and had the privilege to meet with Hong's future father-in-law and know of the custom and tradition in a high class family of Hanoi.

One of our friends Chu-van-Tich became chief of the Information Office. One day of September he asked us to think of something for the kids to celebrate the mid-autumn festival. I said as the French came back to the South we will set up mock things for them to fight the invaders. A small boat will be decorated to look like a French warship sailing on Hoan-Kiem lake. On board will be two or three men dressed like French sailors and when the ship was about to reach the lake shore at a spot with plenty of pomelos skin the kids in processions, drum beat blaring would arrive there throwing those stuffs at it chanting "death to the French". I asked Le-van-De, a well known artist, to suggest decorating the surrounding, Then we strung lights on the trees and along the rooftop of Ngoc-Son temple. That full moon night offered a spectacle of very inspiring dynamism.

During this period there were several instances of assassination and bloody killing of which the most prominent case was the "On-nhu-Hau" villa where it was discovered dozens of mutilated bodies scattered in that nice villa on the elegant Bonifaci street. Out on the streets of Hanoi women carrying baskets and bags busily ran back and forth buying and selling the Chinese notes while there were rumors of the presence of Admiral Thierry d'Argenlieu off the Hai-Phong harbor. In the South the arrival of the British Gracy delegation brought with them the French.

The news created a real shock and the Southerner students got ready to go home fighting the French, repelling the colonialists. The patriotic songs of Luu-huu-Phuoc like Dien-Hong, Bach-dang-Giang, Hung-Vuong and specially the one titled Xep-but-nghien (putting away pens and ink) which was very fitting had strengthened the determination of the boys showing the will to fight on their hardened faces. Among the big group leaving that morning I still remember some prominent names like Huynh-van-Tieng, Dang-ngoc-Tot, Mai-van-Bo, Giang-van-Tung, Nguyen-trung-Trinh, Lam-trong-Thuc.

The Viet-Minh administration was through a very dangerous turmoil. On one side the presence of the Chinese troop brought about a climate of insecurity for the population and they offered a screen for activities of the opposing VNQDD. On the other side the French in the South and the presence of d'Argenlieu off Hai-Phong created heavy diplomatic and military pressures. Then they resorted to the trick of "national alliance". Before year end they set up the national reconciliation and alliance conference in the Ba-Da pagoda of Hoan-Kiem lake. I had the opportunity to be there as member of the students delegation.

We were at the meeting place about ten minutes before Ho-chi-Minh arrived. When the VNQDD delegates came with Nguyen-hai-Than, Vu-hong-Khanh, Nguyen-tuong-Tam, Ho-chi-Minh hurriedly rushed out stretching his arms widely to embrace Nguyen-hai-Than with tearing eyes (crocodile tears). Then we had the union government, Nguyen-hai-Than becoming vice-president, Nguyen-tuong-Tam foreign minister and Vu-hong Khanh chairman of the armed forces commission.

After the Dalat caucus came the Fontainebleau conference, then under the banner of French Union the accord of 6 March was sealed. And the French officially returned. On campus a number of students were selected to wear military uniforms and go to Hai-Phong and ride jeeps bringing the French into the capital city.

As the French were back the Chinese must returh to China and the VNQDD lost back up. The Viet-Minh was then free to liquidate the opposition, surrounding and disbanding the Dai-Viet centers and their military school in Yen-Bai. News leaked out on the savagery in Yen-Bay when they surrounded the school and killed throwing bloody corpses in the tainted red river.

Among the victims were my class mates Dang-van-But and Dang-van-Nghien, the two sons of Mr. Do-quang-Giai, Do-quang-Lung and Do-quang-Hien, A living testimony is the case of my friend Nguyen-dinh-Tu now in Virginia.

His back was cut with machete and he was thrown for dead in the river. Miraculously he was washed ashore regained consciousness and survived the onslaught.

A few of them were able to make their way out to South China and later returned to Hanoi to become prominent civilian and military leaders in South Viet Nam. On campus also occurred the terrible event of a band of hoodlums entering during the wee hours to arrest and blindfold tutor Phan-thanh-Hoa who had since then disappeared. And in our city of Thanh-Hoa they dragged out to the street the manager of our Tu-Dan hotel, Mr. Dang-tran-Ho grand father of Mrs Dang-tuyet-Mai to club him and finally kill him with a shot in his head.

Back to the beginning of 1946 one special event had marked my life for long. In January buddy Nguyen-tan-Hong celebrated his marriage with Miss Vinh, Along with Bui-Diem, Nguyen-mong-Bich and Nguyen-thanh-Huy we were best men. As for maids of honor there were the two nieces Bao and Tram. I liked Bao and went to her home at 153 Hang-Long street where I learned that her father had been incarcerated as a nationalist reactionary in an unknown place. As I knew well Le-van-Lang, a law school student who had become director of the security office I offered my help. I went to Lang's office at Gambetta street and got his promise to look into the matter. And that's why I had valid reasons to come often and I sometimes went out with her biking together to the West or the Truc-Bach lakes. I had to mention here the two mail birds, Tram and Lan who spent their time taking back and forth our love letters. I got the works to Thanh-Hoa to get permission from my parents with the engagements proceedings.

Then one day I went to the Hanoi train station to escort mother and auntie Hien in their rickshaw loaded with all the special presents of Thanh-Hoa like sun dried squids and prawns to 153 Hang-Long street. While I sat down in the living room and had my luncheon with the father-in-law and all the uncles, in the ante room to the ancestors altar four ladies sat crossed legs on a heavy antique platform, covered with a brocade mat, entertaining each other to a sumptuous meal and Bao standing by to wait on them, arms crossed in the traditional posture.

My mother requested an wedding as soon as possible because my grand mother was very sick at the time. But the turn of events with the French had deteriorated so rapidly that things could not be done as wished. And I was unable to go to my grandma burial. Then I was rapidly demoted from the standing of a dignified uncle status to the level of a humble nephew.

During that period there were many incidents between the Vietnamese and the French. Families got instructions to cut open their walls to facilitate a guerilla street war and on campus we also set up a battalion of frontline student fighters. And each and every night I took my guard duty at the small bridge behind the campus dressed in my pajama and my beloved woolen hat, a thick blanket over it and armed with a mousqueton French gun which I had never tried before. And what was expected had come. In the middle of the night the French started firing and conquered the whole Hanoi quickly.

One medical student of reputation, Dr. Nguyen-tai-Chat, was killed on the street while he was trying to assist the wounded dressed in his white medical robe. Chat was the brother-in-law of Madame Phan-huy-Quat and just married to Dang-thi-Tam a few short months ago. The people of Hanoi fled the capital city and went South to the countryside with all means imaginable.

Bao's family went to the village of Dao-Xa of one distant relative. And when the students brigade was disbanded I rejoined them and stayed for a few days sleeping on straw mats before I ventured out to Phu-Ly to seek shelter at Hong's father home. There I learned that the whole family had moved East to the village of Vinh-Tru by boat and I followed suit to stay with them for about ten days before I returned to Dao-Xa to learn of the death of Bao's grandpa being buried in a family lot of the relative. Learning of the French push south, I took everybody to the village of Trieu-Dong and we took shelter with the venerable Nghi Khuong, mother of friend Nguyen-mong-Bich. Trieu-Dong is a typical North Vietnam village surrounded by a thick fence of bamboo trees and the entrance gate is closed shut each night with a night guard who sounded the time regularly with a gong.

We took shelter at Mrs. Nghi Khuong's house, a vast complex housing the ancestral worshipping altar in the middle and all the brick constructions around. About two months later Bao and the family decided to return to Hanoi, a cortege of ragtag people including the young kids of uncle Giap Dung, Hung and Nghia and those of uncle Tu, Dung, Nghi, Diem, Le and Chat. Here I must open a bracket to talk of a very moving spectacle when one witnessed Dung, the oldest sister of the five young orphans squatting on the floor pushing straw into the makeshift kitchen to cook rice while carrying young brother Chat on her lap and the other sisters Nghi, Diem and Le standing by expecting their meal. Dung was eleven, Nghi ten, Diem nine, Le five and Chat merely three. Only the talented pen of Norman Rockwell could truly depict the scene and soul of such a heart breaking sight.

Back to Trieu-Dong I was all by myself. Out of the sorrow of missing my sweetheart my only pastime was to go day in day out to the Dong-Quan market place to eat my daily bowl of beef noodle soup and gather all the news and rumors of the situation. There one day I acquainted with a young man named Su. He was single appeared to have good manners, a very soft speaking and polite guy. He went from Dong-Quan to Cong-Than and Cho-Dai through all those market places wheeling and dealing for commissions and self sustenance.

While having a cup of coffee together I suddenly asked him: "Su, would you have any idea on some very simple things that the people really need now?". He quickly answered from the cuff of his sleeves "worms flushing medicine". It gave me a flashback to a product named "huile de ricin chenopodee", castor oil with chenopodium used to flush earthworms from your entrails.

I then said that if I could buy cold pressed castor oil I could procure some chenopodium essence and easily mix them into the wanted medicine. Su indicated to me that beyond the Red River there was a village which produced hot pressed castor oil to make soap. With my logical thinking it seemed that pressing boiled castor beans would yield more oil than cold pressing the raw beans and it would come down to the price offered.

I asked Su to go along with me armed with a clean kerosene 20 liter tin can, a carrying bamboo pole and rattan harness. When we arrived at the village and after the price was agreed upon I paid them cash in advance and left all our gears before going further in the Southest direction to Khoai-Chau village, the home of roommate Nguyen-duc-Quang. The oldest brother of Quang, Mr. Kinh is a pharmacist making extract of chenopodium there. I asked Mr. Kinh for a liter of the extract and if needed we would hang around for a few days awaiting. Very luckily he had available one liter of the product and I bought it staying just overnight being treated with full fares of chicken over sticky rice and fish rolls before heading back home.

We took delivery of the can of castor oil and carried it to the boat landing to cross the Red River once again. But this time the river was all swollen with very choppy red water under a steady northern wind. The small boat rolled and rocked violently and it took a while to bring us back to the other bank all scared and frozen cold. There would still be 15 kilometers to Trieu-Dong and both of us each one at one end of the long bamboo pole we hauled the heavy castor oil can huffing and puffing through snaking dirt paths and finally reached home at midnight. After proper identification the guard opened the gate for us and we brought the stuff in. I paid Su a fee and promised to see him the next day in Dong-Quan.

I was there quite early and Su was also expecting me. I took him to a coffee shop for a bowl of hot beef noodle soup and told him to try looking for one thousand small glass bottles with cork stoppers while I got busy ordering a rubber stamp to imprint labels. Back to my room I started mixing the ingredients as indicated in details by pharmacist Kinh, affix labels to the small glass jars and during the ensuing days I hauled cases and cases of it to Dong-Quan by small sampans on the canal to the market. To my big and pleasant surprise I disposed of the whole batch in a couple of days owing to the law of supply and demand and moreover to the very clever promotional action of Su. I became cash rich, life was so easy and rosy and I can afford succulent steak and French fries every day.

A few days later Hong and Vinh came up from Phat-Diem. Old chums being together after such a long and uncertain absence it was an endless reminiscence of souvenirs, good and bad ones, things you have been through, hardships you had endured. Then Vinh asked "what shall we do now for a living, we have only a few hundreds piastres in our pocket"? I suggested that Hong and I would go to Dong-Quan for an assessment tour before any decision could be made. There I bought a stall at the center of the place, a small thatched hut with a makeshift counter and bench. I paid for the whole thing having plenty of cold cash in my pocket.

We set up for business and by buying and selling we were able to have enough revenue for our daily food need. One day I saw them selling full cardboard drums of salicylic acid and also at another place they had pure caustic soda for sale. My fast mind kept churning. If we mix those two things together may be we would get salicilate of soda a potent drug for treatment of rheumatoid arthritist disease? Then when I shuffled through a hip of old books and magazines I saw an old beaten up Codex which is the reference guide book of pharmacy and I bought immediately with almost nothing.

Back to our stall I hurriedly looked at salicilate of soda and found the relevant chemical equation. Codex explained that the two ingredients possess opposite but complementary physical properties. While caustic soda is fully soluble in water the other one is insoluble which would facilitate the separation process by filtration. We bought one kilo of each and took home for experimentation. When we put them together in a big ceramic bowl, lo and behold, the violent chemical reaction ensued at once, bubbling sending billowing clouds of steam through the whole room. When it subsided and cooled down we saw rows of pinky fish scales like clinging to the side of the bowl. At touch it felt oily and when I put a tat of it to the tip of my tongue it tasted lightly sweet, exactly as described in the Codex.

The road to riches was only halfway crossed, and the remains were still complex to achieve. The product must be administered by injection only so you have to be certain that it was of relatively good quality. Then you must have pure still water to make the solution and put it in closed glass vials. Thinking of one of our friends pharmacist who was in charge of the military pharmaceutical directorate upland beyond Van-Dinh we wrapped up a ball of the product and sent it to him by special courier with request for a test.

One week later we got his message back with only a short word "pure". I went out buying all kinds of glass bottles and recipients and built my apparatus to make ultra pure water. I sent Su out looking for all the long glass tubes from the stock of the displaced pharmaceutical firms.

With tin cans I fabricated my alcohol blow torch spewing out long extra hot and blue flames to melt and turn those glass tubes into elegant vials. I spent long hours at the job and though at first there were plenty of hits-and-misses for the garbage can I honed my skill and finally I made plenty of uniformed beautiful vials which Hong filled with his injector and Vinh melted shut in a line production scheme.

We loaded the whole batch in a big kettle secured with clothes and towels and no-one-knows-what's, filled with water, boiled and put to simmer overnight. Finally I gave the finishing touch with labels using the rubber stamp and varnish. When displayed in our stall they sold like hotcakes, wholesalers came in force grabbing everything and even agents from the army pharmaceutical directorate came down and gave big orders. The problem now is how to jack up the production line to face such a huge demand. We worked overtime but cash came in big, richness was there, life was so easy and Vinh spent her time sorting, counting and rubber banding all those bank notes.

A couple of months later while I was busy behind the counter a young liaison agent came and gave me a letter from my classmates at the faculty of sciences urging me to join them at the weapons development directorate in Hoa-Binh under the famous polytechnics engineer Tran-dai-Nghia. The young agent was my junior of six years at Khai-Dinh school, the son of Mr. Pham-phu-Tiet vice governor of Thanh-Hoa. He was named Pham-phu-Thanh, nicknamed Lion and had one sister Pham-thi-Xuan-Tho nicknamed Mouse who later was married to Ngo-trong-Anh, minister of public works in Nguyen-cao-Ky cabinet.

As I felt lonesome without Bao I accepted the invitation and with my backpack I biked up North to Hoa-Binh. But when I reached Van-Dinh the French dropped their sticks of paratroopers there and I had to hurry back losing all tracks. It was felt as a bad luck but if I was able to cross the pass to Hoa-Binh my life would have been given a rotation of 180 degrees and I would not know where I would be now. So tough luck turned out to be good fortune!

A good while later on the same young agent came and gave me a message from Nguyen-dinh-Quang, a class mate in Khai-Dinh and in charge of the counter intelligence service asking me to go to Hanoi for a special mission under the code name z-4. As I long for my sweet heart I accepted the offer immediately, que sera sera! I bid farewell to Hong-Vinh leaving to them all the cash and the whole business in full swing went with a female guide, dressed in my clean white shirt and trouser.

When we were about to reach Nga-tu-So I went through the first French checkpoint outpost and the sergeant in charge asked me a few questions on where I was going to and what I intended to do, to that I answered in a good clear French and I was let go without a hitch. There was still fifteen kilometers to 153 Route Mandarine and on a deserted highway I was trotting along gingerly and effortlessly to my beloved destination.

One cannot describe the moving scene of reunion with Bao kissing and sobbing, tearing eyes having never expected such a surprise get together. During this time Bao's mother had opened an alterations shop on Hue street and I became the lead worker pedaling the old Singer machine all day. One funny thing occurred when one day a man brought in a length of cloth to order a shirt custom made. I took his measurements and cut and assembled the shirt but when he came it did not fit and did not even look like a decent work. We had to repay him with cash and plenty of apologies and embarrassments.

When Bao's mom closed the shop I went out to work for Mr. Kim at his identity photo shop near Cua Nam street. I spent all day taking snap shots of the brave lady merchants for their identity cards as required by the authority for access to the city market and worked also in the darkroom. The funny thing was when they got their photos they always complained that while their eyes were normal and healthy it showed a white dot as if they had cataracts. Although I had explained to them that it was the reflection of the light beam in their eye they were not pleased and I finally had to use black ink to fix those spots.

I received the first assignment from the counter intelligence service: I had to do the impossible to go into the French Artillery Citadel and get rough indications on the number of workers going in every morning as long as the number of military trucks available. With those raw and rough data they could estimate the amplitude of the next French operation.

That morning I rode my bicycle out very early to Duviliers Street and commingling with the big crowd of workers I went through the gate, moving back and forth in the vast complex and went out with the crowd at noon break time. It was a big surprise to me that I went through the whole venture without any problem.

As directed I wrote down the two numbers on a piece of candy wrapper, crumbled it and threw at the base of a tree in front of Mr. Do-quang-Tri's shop. After a short stroll when I returned to the same spot the crumbled wrapper was gone.

A short time later I received the visit of another spy agent who then showed me a square pack of opium resin and asked for my help to sell them because "out there our brothers need cash". That was it, I decided to find ways and get out of the dragnet.

One day while on my way to work I came across with Dang-van-Sung. He stopped his bike and asked whether I still had enthusiasm and if yes he urged me to move in with him. I packed my belongings and moved to 68 Reinach street which he had rented from Mrs. Phan-huy-Quat.

I was referred by Dr. Sung to Miss Rosa Minh, director of social services and went to work for her as chief of the honor loan department to refugees. A few months later I went to the US consulate general to apply for a scholarship in America in the same time than the other buddies Nguyen-dinh-Hoa, Vu-tam-Ich and Dang-the-Binh. But I was not eligible because I wanted to do mechanical engineering while the scholarships offered were only for linguistics, economics and social studies.

Then we decided to set our marriage proceedings revving. There was a big reception at 68 Reinach with the presence of all the top brass of Hanoi, the mayor of Hanoi Phan-xuan-Dai, the vice governor of North Viet Nam Vu-quy-Mao, the director of social services Rosa Minh. Corks of bottles of French Champagne Moet and Chandon kept popping owing to the help of uncle Truc, a sales manager for the French company Denis Freres.

On wedding day April 17th of 1949 we used three big American cars graciously lent by uncle Truc and another friend Vu-van-Khoa. The cortege went to the bride's home with the groom dressed in black woolen pants and white crossed lapels coat being escorted by the two best men Le-van-Nham who later became a prominent eye doctor in Paris and Nguyen-dinh-Tu now in Virginia. After lengthy rituals we took the bride home dressed in her crimson brocade gown with a garland of flowers on her head and surrounded by four beautiful maids of honors, preceded by the 10 years old flowers girl Tu-Anh. Across street three young girls Thinh, Son and Dai watched the scene in admiration.

When Dr. Nguyen-ton-Hoan became minister of sport and youth I was his director of sport and physical education. Then the central government planned to move south and I volunteered to be with the first group to go to Saigon and get things settled. We moved into 185 Mayer street which was to be the residence of the minister. As there was not yet separate office place for the organization we lived upstairs and set up desks and equipment in the very limited space downstairs. Along with Nguyen-dinh-Tu and Nguyen-tat-Ung we worked downstairs and after hours we went up, eating at the same table than Dr. Hoan's family and sleeping on the bare tiled floor.

There I learned of a very moving love story of Hoan and his wife Binh. While Hoan was in South China with the expatriate Dai-Viet group Mrs Hoan joined the resistance in the South fighting the French invaders. The resistance then sent her back to Saigon with a very special and clear mission to either convince Hoan to go with the resistance or execute him on the spot with a small pistol she had with her. After a long night talking and sobbing filled with plenty of tears the reversed decision was made, Binh was convinced by her husband to stay with the nationalist cause.

The youth ministry opened a training school for future cadres of sport and youth in Nha-Trang, somewhat along the model of the French ESEPIC (ecole superieure d'education physique de l'Indochine) under Commandant Ducouroy.We had very good instructors, Le-Ninh and Duong-ngoc-Cong for sports and physical education, Tran-van-Thao for youth activities and as far as military training was concerned there were Nguyen-dinh-Tu, Vu-duc-Hai, Tran-thanh-Dam, Dang-van-De, survivors of the Dai-Viet military school when attacked en masse by the Viet-Minh.

One day per week I flew to Nha-Trang to give lectures on sport medicine. Then I had the opportunity to enjoy the blue water and the white sand beach and eat those very tasty and fresh seafood dishes cooked on the beach. Well those foods could be very appetizing and succulent but they were not healthy and sanitary enough so that I had contracted typhoid fever which almost killed me.

Among the trainees who were afterwards sent to the Dalat military school some had become brilliant soldiers of South Vietnam like Generals Do-kien-Nhieu, Tran-van-Hai, Ma-sanh-Nhon, Huynh-van-Ton, etc…

In March I was getting ready to take my family to Saigon. I had rented a place at 117 Legrand de la Liraye street and upon reference by Ung, Mr. Duc owner of a furniture shop in Gia-Dinh had custom made for me one bed with nightstands, a dining set with eight chairs, an armoire and a divan. He charged me very reasonably and let me pay him by installments.

I got the good news to Hanoi but her mom had not wanted to let her daughter go thinking that with the first childbirth she would need to be close to mommy for assistance. Afterwards as recounted by Bao she went through a very rough and dangerous time but owing to the help of the good doctor Patterson and the constant care given by her mom she was able to make it through the ordeal.

In the mean time the house became a transient place for all the friends like Nguyen-dinh-Tu, Nguyen-tat-Ung, Pham-Chu, Pham-trong-Nhan, Dang-van-De, eating and resting at will. Some nights on the only bed four or five guys lied down head to toes for a good sleep. Every evening, dressed in well pressed shirts and pants, adorned with colorful bowties they hired special taxi cabs and headed for the Arc-en-Ciel dancing hall for a fun filled evening till the wee hours. At that time the northerners boys looked down on the shabbily dressed Southerners in their traditional vestments although awash of cash!

In May only Bao came down carrying the short lived Hung-Phong bringing peace and quietness to the house. Then my mother and the three youngest brothers Hoang, Cam and Thien came from Thanh-Hoa and a couple of months later my father rejoined with the other two Loc and Hoa. After so many years of separation I felt very happy and blessed and though our means were very limited Bao had all the courage to provide as much as we could. In February little Hung-Phong suddenly fell ill and was admitted into Grall hospital for treatments. I worried so much that I spent all my time there not letting Bao coming because she was near childbirth. Each and every day I went to the hospital church to kneel down praying for protection from the compassionate Saint Mary. Then on 12 February Phong died and on the same day Bao gave birth to our daughter Thanh-Huong. When I buried Phong at the North Vietnam cemetery I cried my heart off and fell into the dug hole and the friends Ung and Tu had to pull me out.

My parents-in-law circa 1944

The newly weds, 04-17-1949

CHAPTER THREE

III.-Life twists and turns

There were changes in the government. Premier Tran-van-Huu took over from Nguyen-phan-Long and Minister Hoan was replaced by Pham-van-Binh. Then came Minister Nguyen-thanh-Giung, secretary of education cumulatively in charge of youth and sports affairs. Mr. Giung was a well known and respected professor at the lycees Chasseloup Laubat and Petrus Ky. He decided to let me go along with the Vietnamese team to the 15th Olympiad in Helsinki, Finland as a special advisor.

The team leaders were all French educated gentlemen like Mr. Nguyen-phuoc-Vong director of Air Vietnam, Judge Tran-van-Thoan, lawyer Huynh-xuan-Canh, Doctor Pham van Phan and professor Nguyen-van-Dau who were fluent French speakers but had very limited English knowledge.

We arrived in Helsinki after two nights in Paris and took our places in the assigned modern and brand new Olympic village. On the first night a very hilarious thing occurred. One of our athletes, a velodrome cyclist of a quite heavy build went to the restroom for his need. Being used to squat Turkish style on the toilet in Saigon he squarely put his feet on the toilet seat and squatted down. But very unluckily he slipped and fell slamming his 180 lbs weight down splitting the toilet bowl with his hand bloodied by a sharp shark of the porcelain fixture. The advisor was busy with his English calling the ambulance to take our man for emergency treatments at the village hospital and coordinating with the village maintenance department for cleanup and installation of a brand new toilet bowl.

A very moving scene was when our marathon runner Tran-van-Ly emerged into the stadium, pale and breathless way behind the whole group who had reached the arrival mark long before, the whole stadium stood up to give a long roaring ovation to a lone Ly staggering along to the final line.

When I came home at the end of September I found two very important papers on my desk. The first one was a summons from the mobilization department asking me to go to the office of military recruitment for induction. The second one was an invitation from Chief of State Bao-Dai to a reception in honor of the returning Vietnam Olympic team.

At the time we had a new Minister of sports Vu-hong-Khanh who, being a senior member of the VNQDD had spent most of his life in exile in South China. He spoke Vietnamese with a heavy Chinese accent like the Chinese in Cholon and his entourage always discussed things in Chinese parley.

Much disappointed with the feeling that my future here was no longer promising, I decided not to sign a request of deferment and went straight to the military recruitment office in Chi-Hoa. There I met an old NCO in charge who coolly with a nod of his head directed me to an adjacent room to sign for a paraphernalia of military stuffs, army fatigues, boots, cigarettes packs and soap cakes etc., in a duffel bag.

One week later on a Friday evening I went to the reception given by Bao-Dai. It was at the big hall of Gia-Long palace and all the cream of the Saigon intelligentsia, the powerful French and Vietnamese VIP's were there chatting and sipping their drinks pending the arrival of Bao-Dai descending with majesty the huge staircase under crimson carpet. I felt lost in the big crowd of dignitaries when at a sudden Premier Nguyen-van-Tam the well known "grey tiger of Cai-Lay" came to me and shook my hand saying "I have two things to commend you young man: first you had fulfilled beautifully your task in Helsinki, second you had volunteered to join the army. If there is anything I can help, let me know".

I said: "Sir joining the Army is my responsibility. But having a family with almost two kids and being a civil servant under contractual obligation I will not get a differential pay like the regular government functionary. My family economic situation would be very difficult". Then premier Tam suddenly raised his hand waiving and shouting "sonny, general Nguyen-van-Hinh". The general rushed to his father and both men spoke to each other in French a few steps from where I stood.

About one minute later General Hinh. A ramrod soldier with tanned complexion walked to me and said "come to see me at my office on Galieni Boulevard next Monday at 10 a.m." On the day, dressed in suit and tie I entered his office and was greeted by Lieutenant Tran-van-Don (later became Major General and Defense Minister) who steered me to General Hinh's bureau. After showing me a chair in front of him the General went straight into the matter: " I have seen your file, you got a couple of certificate of mathematics at the Hanoi faculty of sciences. I'd not let you go to Thu-Duc. Instead of you'll go to France to attend the French Air Academy of Salon de Provence. Any questions"? Then

I said can I take pilot training , to it he firmed his voice "no you are too old to be a pilot, you will be air mechanical engineer".

Before dismissing me he gave me a piece of paper telling me to get ready for the October 1953 class. When I got into my car I looked at the paper and to my big surprise it was the decree signed by Nguyen-van-Tam giving me the rank of second lieutenant to go for study at the French Air Academy in France. It was a double rewards, I fulfill my dream to go abroad for further study and my wife will have enough income to take care of the family. I told my driver to go back straight to the Chi-Hoa Military recruitment office to return the duffel bag which was still in the trunk of the car. When he saw me the same old NCO raised his whimsical eyes and when I gave him the decree he suddenly stood up giving me a stiff military salute, knocking his boots together and said "Sir, please leave everything here, have a nice trip to France and I'll take care of every needed paper works during your absence".

In mid August I boarded the Air France Sky Master flight to France. Bao with her six month-baby-bearing-bulging-belly carrying Huong on one hand while wrapping her other arm around me cried tears running down her cheeks but determined to accept the sacrifice for the sake of the future in the traditional oriental tradition. The Air France plane had four propeller driven engines, slow speed and could not go straight to France. It had to make stops on the way for refueling and check up. In the passengers lounge I saw a small group of young Vietnamese boys all pale and weary looking. I only knew afterwards that they also went to Salon after a tight examination in Saigon.

We landed at Nice and then proceeded to Le Bourget airport of Paris where a military bus took us to the transit military center to stay for five days before going south. This was my second encounter with Paris and as I had plenty of time I could get in touch with my brother in law studying here since 1950. Every day we strolled in the Latin Quarter, sipped our demi tasses at the Boulevard coffee shops, visited the manicured garden of Luxembourg with the well known statue of the thinker by Rodin, the baroque small theaters, the elegant and tall Eiffel tower, the medieval bridges studded with statues, the massive cathedral of Notre Dame of Paris taking me back to the masterpiece of Victor Hugo with Esmeralda and the humpback of Notre Dame, the elaborate and imposing Arch of Triumph in the center of the elegant Champs Elysees.

Wow! All those monumental works of art which had been embedded in my mind since the days in high school and now unfurling before my own eyes as if leafing through an old textbook giving me the most powerful impression of the French cultural heritage. Then I boarded the train going South at the station Gare du Nord. I met Dang-dinh-Linh a few years junior to me and going also to Salon de Provence. During the long train ride we talked of so many things and I befriended right away with that soft spoken and mild mannered young man.

When we arrived at Salon de Provence an air force van took us to the air base adjutant office where they issued French Air Force uniforms and the first pay check counting from our first day of enlistment. With the base pay rate of a French lieutenant plus all the various allocations, family allowances, housing and expatriation pay, it was much better than what I used to get while with the sport ministry in Saigon. And we learned that officers would live off base then along with Linh we rented a place downtown at the home of a widow lady living with her teenage daughter.

We bought Mobilettes to move around and every day we went through the main street on our way to school, passing in front of the Mossy Fountain where underground water cascaded down for a few hundred years, the bell tower gate leading to the ancient home of Nostradamus and the museum of the Emperi displaying all the artifacts of Napoleon's army and empire.

The roadway to the school went through about 15 kilometers of winding thoroughfare lined with old twisted trees. Salon de Provence is blessed with a mild climate with clear blue sky most of the times except for about two or three days of fluttering snow during winter. But during that season there were often cases when the Mistral started blowing whipping with more than 90 miles spikes of furious wind it then became miserably freezing. I remember one day when Linh and I were steadily going to school the gusty Mistral suddenly blew and lifted us off the ground throwing us violently against a tree to fall face down, hat and school work books scattered everywhere. Then we got up, crawling and clawing and seeing that we had no major injuries except for a few minor cuts and scratches we gathered all our stuff, restarted our mopeds and proceeded to school as if nothing had happened but a little bit scared!

We belonged to 53 EIM brigade (eleve ingenieur mecanicien) with around 35 French students and six Vietnamese under the command of captain de Rauglaude. Linh and I having officers ranks were authorized to live off base, the others guys were in board cadets and subjected to strict military training and to the traditional hazing imposed by the upper class students. The main edifice of the academy was the BDE (building des eleves), an imposing construction looking like an old castle with five stories and off limit to all cadets except during the year end Grand Ball.

It was also the headquarters of the commanding general and his staff.

The Grand Ball was a very special event and the whole city of Salon de Provence went through a high state of fever during the few months preceding the show. All families having teenage daughters did the impossible to get invitation for them to be escorted to the Grand Ball by cadets dressed in their summer white uniforms, immaculate gloves and with their short dragonne sword dangling along their left side. The girls in their long and elaborately appointed robes would go in, hand under arm of the boys climbing the several steps to the main lobby as dainty and elegant as in the scenes of turn of the century Royal festivities.

They had orchestras playing on each floor to a different tune, romantic tangos on the first floor, swirling waltz on the second floor, passionate latin music cha cha, sambas and rumbas on the third floor and finally the frenetic rock music on the top floor, accommodating each and everyone's taste and energy as time went by fast until the wee hours when the party came suddenly to a close.

I had acquainted with the owners of a sport store on the main street where I often bought my sport accessories. They had a daughter of eighteen years old and asked whether I would invite her to the Grand Ball. I accepted the offer and that night the shop owner chauffeured us to the brightly illuminated BDE where I was the only Vietnamese to elegantly escort a blond French girl up the stairs dressed in her very beautiful evening dress training on the stair steps to the dancing lobby.

Back to our school, engineering students went to class at a row of classrooms and machine shops under the direction of several university professors coming from Marseille and

Aix en Provence. Each week the school bus took us to the shops of the college of Arts and Metiers of Aix to hone our skills in shop works. We daily ate at the school mess hall, a spacious building with square dining tables having four chairs each. As we lived off base we only had breakfast and lunch there.

They always had at each table one liter of red wine and a round Camembert cheese piece at all regular meals. At first the Vietnamese did not like them and always traded them with the French boys for other things but after several weeks they gradually became accustomed to the taste and then started to gulp their red wine with bites of Camembert and French bread.

After a few days tailors were sent to the school to take measurements for our custom made summer white uniforms and winter dark blue outfits including a thick woolen overcoat. And two weeks later came the important and pompous ceremony of dragonne sword remittal amid military band playing and troops review on the football size reviewing ground in front of the BDE with the presence of all the generals coming from other bases. Then on the last week of November we had the visit of our Minister of Defense Phan-huy-Quat accompanied by his aide Bui-Diem. After talking to all the Vietnamese students he gave me the special honor of a special one on one interview but that was why I was labeled as an important member of the Dai-Viet group.

On Christmas Linh and I went to Spain. I got a room at a pensione de familia in Barcelona and before going down by train I bought a book to learn some basic Spanish conversational words. The house was located on a quaint winding street but very close to the main Plaza de Cataluna and every night we went out there mixing with the male crowd, clapping hands and stepping to the joyful pasadoble music blared from the speakers around the place.

I had to say that the social custom here at present time was of a male dominated society, with women toiling at home, cleaning, laundering, ironing and cooking while the males spent their time doing their nails care and going out dancing and singing to their heart pleasure. The meal schedule was also very odd, breakfast at 11 am, lunch at around 5 pm and dinner or supper at almost midnight. That was why every night after dinner we went out to the central plaza having fun and stayed in bed until very late next morning for our breakfast.

Barcelona had so many astounding monuments like the half completed Church of the Sagrada Familia by a famous architect. Around the plaza de Cataluna there were rows of fashionable boutiques and shops selling very finely crafted leather goods.

On the New Year's eve they organized a dance party and we were invited to join in, changing partners every fifteen minutes at a knock on the floor by the master of ceremony. Close to the final hour each male dancer was given a small paper bag containing grapes and when the clock started sounding the final hour of the year each man had to swallow or chew all the grapes until the last chime and then would be permitted to kiss whatever partner he was dancing with, laughing and applauding to the customary wish of Buenos Anos.

At the Easter Holiday we went with the whole class to the ski resort of Ancelles in the Alps. We were given skis and various accessories and we learned skiing under the supervision of instructors. After a few days of falling and slipping I finally was able to glide about faster and effortlessly.

When descending a slope I hit a tree stump buried under the snow and fell rolling many times head to toe to end up landing face down, eagle spread, my left foot twisted completely off to the other direction and my ankle puffed up like an elephant leg. Hearing my call for help the instructor skied down in a hurry, took the skis off and brought me on a stretcher to a near by sanatorium for urgent care. The first thing they did was trying to straighten my left foot to its normal position. They used an injection needle as big as a nail to administer pain killer all around my ankle and tried to turn my foot straight back. Then I was transported down to a military hospital in Marseille where I stayed for almost a month, leg in plaster cast and hung to the ceiling with sling and pulley.

I felt so depressed and lonesome and one day I gave three light knocks on the adjacent wall and to my surprise I heard a few scratches on the other side of the wall. So an unintelligible line of communication was established filling my loneliness with hope and expectations. Then I decided to give a short written message of introduction to the nurse on duty asking her to remit to the unknown patient next door. To my surprise I received the answer back in no time telling that her name was Monique and she was an auxiliary air force person having a broken pelvis bone when she slipped and fell on the icy sidewalk of Marseille.

And so our messages flew back and forth and we became friends without knowing each other' s faces and promised to meet the day of our discharge. That day finally came and on that sunny and nice morning I went out with crutches under both arms and Monique, a red head girl, was there with a walking cane in her hand and both of us sat on the bench talking and talking until the school van took me back to Salon de Provence. Being away from school for nearly a month it took me lots of effort and work to finally catch up with my classmates.

The summer vacation started on mid June and Commandant Grolleau and his wife came to take me out for a tour of the Loire Valley. Commandant Grolleau was formerly an assistant to Commandant Ducouroy at the sports department of Governor General Decoux. He had become advisor to our Minister of sports and youth but was a special friend of mine treating me like his own son. Mr and Mrs Grolleau drove me to see the whole Loire Valley for one week, visiting every beautiful castle built along the river and when we arrived at Rennes we stayed there overnight and I had the chance to taste raw fresh oysters sipping along the finest French white wine Muscadet.

Back to Salon de Provence I went with Linh to Nice, staying for two weeks in the villa for officers visiting the many beautiful places like Saint Jean Cap Ferrat, Cannes, Frejus, Antibes, Monte Carlo, etc… This villa was donated by Empress Josephine to the officers of the army of Emperor Napoleon as an R and R place. It was free of charge to all transient officers and each morning we had waiters bringing continental breakfasts ceremoniously to our bed.

When we were back home we changed our address to 13 Labadie street of Mme Laugier living there with her only daughter, an old maid Miss Eliette Laugier. In 1995 during one of our trips to France I have taken Bao along to show her my former school and we had a very warm welcome by the General commanding the base who hosted us at a nice luncheon at the Club for Generals and afterwards pinned the poussin's insignia on Bao's lapel.

We went afterwards looking for my former shelter at 13 Labadie. Things looked unchanged but when we knocked at the pinkish entrance door with no answer a neighbor lady showed up and wondered whether I was one the Vietnamese guys that Mrs Laugier always talked of with emotional reminiscence. I said yes and was told that Mme Laugier passed away long ago while her daughter Eliette was in the hospital having her legs amputated. I got her room number at the hospital and we brought a bouquet along to pay Eliette a surprise visit. On her sick bed Eliette looked much older but she recognized me right away asking us how many kids we had to that I answered sixteen to the clear bewilderment of the old woman: Having not used any French for so long I mistook the work grandkids for grown up children!

Back to that summer, I bought from Nguyen-ngoc-Loan his brand new dark blue convertible Peugeot 203. Loan being a single man and getting his flight pay as a first lieutenant he had plenty of cash to spend. He had the character of a shoot-from-the-hip guy, acting always at the whim of the moment He bought that car, had fun with it for about three weeks before he felt tired of and gave the word out that he would resell it for one third of his cost. So I caught the opportunity right away and from then on Linh and I sold our mobilettes and we could commute to school without any fear of the gusty Mistral. And we also had the possibility to go around, visiting the many places like Avignon, Marseille, Montpellier, Aix, Grenoble and Lyon, etc…

In October of 1953 I got news from home of the birth of Bich-Thuy, my second princess, "mother round and baby square" as they said. The school adjutant office cut a new pay check with increased family allowances. I must mention here that now and then I received additional checks which I did not know why and I finally got used to it and stopped bothering about it. At that time there was the "traffic of the piasters" and I had been approached too. I'd give my French Francs to a designated person here and in Saigon they'd pay my wife with piasters at a much higher rate than the official one. And there each family member was given a postal transfer card authorizing you to buy and send 7,000 francs at the official rate of exchange. So the money kept rolling in yielding more revenue for Bao to take care of supporting a big family including my young brothers who rejoined us from Thanh-Hoa.

The second school year came at a blink of your eyes. I was selected to go with a few French cadets to the University of Marseille to attend the class of Fluids Mechanics. Each and every week the school van took you twice to Marseille to attend the class and do works at the Wind Tunnel.

On Christmas 1954 an old Saigon French boy scout friend graciously invited me to join his family at their apartment in the ninth arrondissement of Paris. After a warm Christmas eve party his parents decided to go to their daughter place out of town and gave me the keys urging me to feel at home during their absence. It was a very rare occasion for me to really enjoy a vacation in Paris without strings, free to go here and there, sitting at length in those cafes de boulevard, people watching sipping my demi-tasses.

At night I'd go to the Left-Bank and enjoyed my most flavorful steaks with French fries or standing in the shivering cold next to the grill eating their fresh roasted chestnuts. Each morning I'd go down very early to the corner street bakery and buy the crusty French baguette fresh off the oven, had them split, insert ham with butter spread and enjoyed my delicious breakfast with a hot cup of café-au-lait.

My class work went on smoothly, I had all straight A's, and life kept moving on without hitch like clockwork. Nevertheless news of war from home had not been so rosy. The French army had many losses at Hoa-Binh and Cao-Bang, our Vietnamese troops were having a very difficult time in the delta of North Vietnam. The French government sent their most brilliant General De Lattre De Tassigny to take command of the French Expeditionary Corps.

Then De Lattre went to America seeking unsuccessfully assistance, and Bernard his only son was killed at Ninh Binh. We were only disturbed by the bad news a little bit while sitting around the tables in the mess hall. But things quickly returned to normalcy until the news of the critical Dien-Bien-Phu battle came out when the Viet-Minh had the direct assistance of communist China. Then Dien-Bien-Phu fell with General de Castries and thousands of his men taken prisoners, a very bad news giving us a mixed feeling, proud of the Vietnameses defeating the French and worries at the dangers of communism.

In the mess hall although there were no explicit comments, the atmosphere was simply insipid. Among the French boys there was a subdue attitude, no more dirty words, no more yelling and profanities, while at the Vietnamese tables one could only hear low key discussions with some furtive eyes.

I had no worries since my family and parents were in Saigon but for some boys from Hanoi it was really matter for intense concern. Then the armistice was signed and the country was split into two parts and there were time limits for those willing to go South. Ngo-dinh-Diem took control and by a referendum he deposed Bao-Dai, and started his operation to disband the sects and the Binh-Xuyen group, throwing Saigon into turmoil.

My family had to take shelter for a few days in Phan-Thiet where my father was a school master.

Back to school the program had become more and more difficult. At each weekend the in board cadets were permitted to go out, dressed in their full uniforms and entered the crowded restaurants. This year the French boys became ADL and got a fatter pay check than when they were in PDL (PDL stands for in the legal period while ADL is beyond the legal period, and legal period is the formal time of required military service).

I always went to Marseille to attend class and had more experimental works at the Wind Tunnel, studying the flow of air around the wings and the body of the aircraft and starting to check the air flow through the turbine of the jets engines. In Christmas we had wanted to visit Italy and Rome but as it would be too costly we decided to go back to Paris by train. I did not dare to drive my car, not being familiar with the streets there and it would be easier to use the metro which was a faster and more convenient way to move around in Paris. This time I came across with Nguyen-van-Sau, a tennis champion and formerly a member of the Department of Sport under Minister Pham-van-Binh. Sau had an apartment in Paris and he invited me to join him for a trip to Dauville with a few friends. We went back to Paris the next night through the West Tunnel and our car skidded turning head to tail and we almost died in that accident at the same spot where princess Diana was killed later on.

Back to Salon , with Linh we went again to Nice enjoying the elegant setting of the officers villa and having my own car this time we were able to move around visiting all the famous places of Provence.

During the Easter Holiday I was invited by another former Saigon French boy scout friend to stay at his parents' villa in Cannes. It was a very elegant little place located just across from the beach and every day I went out sun bathing but the beach had pebbles soiled with black oil. On the Easter eve they drove me up hill through a very winding dangerous road to their chalet to attend a very warm and hospitable family dinner showing me that in high class French society there were still very tight family relationships.

After the Holidays I went back to my school, well tanned by the wind and sun of the Riviera but feeling very healthy I was all eager to do my class works. At the start of that summer break I drove off to Grenoble sight seeing. The city was such a beautiful place, the food was different from Provence's but the people seemed cooler and less communicative.

In August we had order to return to Saigon ASAP. Though I was intensely getting ready to pass the examination for the certificate of fluids mechanics at the Faculty of Sciences in Marseille next September, I decided to drop everything off, liquidating all my things, selling my 203 Peugeot to be ready to return to Saigon the soonest for a reunion with my family which was my foremost desire. Madame Laugier and her daughter treated me to a very special Provencal dinner with red wine that she had made herself with grapes grown on her country side cabanon.

In French Cadet Uniform, 10-53

CHAPTER FOUR

IV.- A new opportunity

I bid farewell to Provence, Paris and France. I had loved French culture but I had not been so tickled with France to say that every French thing was good. Now I am looking forward to the future with the hope that I could bring all my know how, be them taught at the school or through personal observations to whatever responsibility I'd be called upon to assume. Back to Saigon on the first week of September I presented myself to Major Tran-van-Ho, Air assistant to the General Chief of the Army General Staff (our air force had not become a separate force). Major Ho assigned me to the job of assistant chief of staff for technical services, a still vague responsibility and in conflict with the directorate of air technical services at the Ministry of Defense. Out of a few observation squadrons using the very antiquated Morane planes all others units like transport, fighters, helicopters and the Bien-Hoa air depot were still pending the transfer over from the French.

I had a French advisor, Commandant Esteve, a fat round belly man, always sweating heavily, but having a good heart and was fully aware of the situation. And an American advisor, Major Brown, was assigned, stiff in his well starchy ironed uniform, and looking quite handsome. I was sandwiched between the two men, completely different in character and methodology, and I had to navigate between the two cleverly and diplomatically to avoid and defuse conflicts. Finally the atmosphere had become more friendly and I ended up some nights at Major Brown's villa sipping scotch with commandant Esteve or at other times at Commandant Esteve's residence gulping red wine with Brown.

One night at the French mess both men chug-a-lugged and became so drunk that I had to chauffeur safely every one home with the American car of Major Brown. After one week of work setting up my offices and assigning new persons to their related tasks I joined the flight crew in a 5 day training C-47 flight by the French Senegal group with a French Captain as aircraft commander and Captain Nguyen-cao-Ky as his co-pilot.

As the C-47 had only a maximum range of seven hours the flight plan was made accordingly Saigon-Clark Field-Okinawa-Tokyo and vice versa. The first leg was uneventful and we stayed overnight in Clark Base to pursue our second leg Clark-Okinawa, taking off close to noon time. Mid way we encountered very stormy weather, rain entering our cargo compartment and flowing on the floor like in a storm drain. We had strong head wind and the aircraft shook and rolled and at the end of seven hours we were still fighting our way ahead.

When we landed at Okinawa we taxied on the runway amid a swarm of fire trucks and ambulances and then we stopped dead mid way running out of gas. A tractor pulled the plane to the parking, had it refueled and inspected before the takeoff to Tokyo. This leg was all routine and we landed at Haneda field, Tokyo very early in the morning.

It was a very long drive to Tokyo and along the route we saw that there were still rows of temporary shelters built with card boards, plywood from crates or corrugated rusty roofing pieces. After a sad heart rending surrender ten years ago Japan was still very poor. But nearly three decades later it suddenly emerged as an economic superpower owing to the discipline of its people and also under the visionary general McArthur they had accepted with courage all political changes to a royal constitutional regime under the power of law.

We stayed for three days in Akasaka Hotel, went shopping in Shinzuku, visiting the red light district to see that the Japanese maids had accepted the shameful way with a smile on their lips but still looking ahead at the future rebuilding their families. I bought two small kimonos to Huong four and Thuy three. At home Huong was dressed in her pink one while Thuy worn her red kimono, proudly standing in front of the doorway to the admiration of others kids of the neighborhood. Thuy having a strong character stood in front of Huong as if she was providing protection to her sister.

My job was not that complex and difficult. It was mainly to set up all offices and desks, defining related responsibilities and limits and assigning subordinates to their tasks. I was lucky to have a team of young men devoid of preconceived ideas, not fearful of changes and eager to go ahead under my leadership. The technical documents on hand were either too old or not updated.

Working with the American counterparts we ordered new TO's (technical orders) related to aircrafts on hand and those to be transferred from the French. We proceeded to change our technical working method from the French way to the American way. I had to say that the French method here was dictated by their lack of parts with the huge demand of war so they had to use their so called system D (debrouiller or do as you can) with lots of cannibalizations to send aircraft aloft, disregarding all standard operation procedures.

The hangars and shops were a complete mess, their floor dirty with a thick crust of grease needing a thorough scraping and clean up. The tool kits issued to mechanics under their liabilities had tools missing or broken. I decided to issue new kits in exchange for the old ones without any charge. My men got busy writing and printing word cards for maintenance and repair for each type of aircraft which were standard procedures for mechanics to use. We pushed for the set up of maintenance docks for each aircraft components and the availability of related spare parts and tools to be positioned nearby at a semi circle bin in front of the repair mechanic in charge, just improving efficiency, precision and output using the Taylor method as well as time and motion study.

On the first week of April the US invited a delegation of five air force officers to an inspection tour of America going through several US air bases. Major Ho directed Major Nguyen-ngoc-Oanh to lead a team including Captain Le-trung-Truc chief of staff, Captain Dang-dinh-Dang deputy chief of staff for personnel, captain Trinh-hao-Tam of the transport group and myself deputy chief of staff materiel to be promoted to a temporary rank of captain.

At that time our air force did not have a special uniform and still used the kaki uniform of the army and I had to borrow from Le-Ninh of the army general staff his gabardine costume. At our arrival at San Francisco airport we were greeted by Major Miller a one time air attaché in Saigon. Major Miller became our escort officer during the whole tour and he informed us that we were treated as brigadier generals traveling by air on a VIP T-29 and while on the ground we would use staff cars displaying one star plates. The visit tour lasted almost one month and ended up with a reception at the Pentagon hosted by the three star judge advocate general.

Back home we foresaw the transfer over from the French the C-47's of their Group Senegal to become our first Transport Group, then the F8F bearcats to our first Fighter Squadron and the Park of Bien Hoa to become our air force depot along with the offices, shops and hangars. After the officers villas in Tan-son-Nhut were given to us I got a villa close to the base gate and after clean up I moved my family on base, relinquishing the rental place in town which had become too crowded with my big family.

Commandant Esteve then helped me buy a Citroen car from the stock they auctioned out at dirt prices. And that was the second car of my life. As said above all aircraft transferred from the French were old or in dire need of service. I went on to schedule our C-47's for IRAN (inspection and repair as necessary) in Clark Field. During the first few ones I had to accompany the flight crew to coordinate fully with the repair facilities at that USAF base.

The work load was quite heavy but everything was executed harmoniously to my satisfaction. Then our air force became a separate entity from the army. Lieuteunant Colonel Ho became our first VNAF commander and I was assigned as his DCS Materiel having under me the offices of technical services, logistical and transport services and construction and engineering services. Our uniforms changed from the kaki color to a light blush blue, our emblems displaying an eagle opening his wings ready to soar.

All of a sudden an unknown lieutenant instructor of the Nha-Trang Air Training School was assigned to replace Ho and quickly promoted to Lieutenant Colonel. It was Nguyen-xuan-Vinh a graduate of the Salon de Provence promotion Brunswick 53 like me. He was a small man rather ugly looking displaying a bumpy reddish face with a pair of big eyes like ready to jump out of their sockets. Sitting at his new big commander desk he gave the impression of a toad prepared to spring out of his hole. Vinh had a good academic background, was a very ambitious man and prepared to make his way up through political maneuverings. While in Nha-Trang he befriended Do-khac-Mai, an insipid observer and Can-Lao rep at the air force.

Mai introduced Vinh to Ngo-dinh-Can the powerful little brother of President Ngo-dinh-Diem and then on his future was sealed. Vinh made Mai his Chief of staff and one could see a small desk set up in the hangar of the Liaison Group of Major Pham-ngoc-Sang for officers to sign up on the roster of the Can-Lao party.

When one guy dropped by my desk wondering why they did not see me signing the paper my answer was clear cut "I intend to serve my Air Force and my country only and not any party. If I was a partisan I'd have joined the Viet-Minh long time before".

That was why I was sent to America to attend the Squadron Officers School in Maxwell Field, Alabama in April 1959. During that time to send someone to training abroad was a very clever way to get rid of the unwanted. I had outstanding grades in school, was graduated at the end of July and ready to go home when I got order from VNAF to stay on and go to Chanute Field, Illinois to another class in industrial management.

Seeing now clearly the purpose behind the action of my superior I decided to dig further and make additional researches in the management techniques and try to get extra know how on other things which could become my left hand skills to use as necessary.

I was lucky to come across with two former advisors who had become my good friends in Saigon, Colonel Carl W. Elder and Major Jasper de Simone. They took me to visit those modern pig farms, Ms Elder taught me the techniques of dress making, using the standard patterns, the various accessories and supplies. The de Simones took me to a construction site where their friends, husband and wife were building their own dream house during their off time.

I finally returned home at the end of November with a ton of new management skills ready to use in my next technical assignment. But to my disappointment I was given a desk job with the title of assistant to the chief of staff, a non existent position according to the organization chart of the VNAF, with not a single detail of job description and responsibility. In our parlance it was a "sit down to have fun and drink tea" assignment to do all miscellaneous works as needed by the chief, away from any connection with any units, that is to say that they were afraid of my possible action to coordinate any possible coup-d'etat in the future.

I was given the task of editing the report written in French (a flat French of the college years) by colonel Hoang-van-Lac on the Strategic Hamlets project to be submitted to President Ngo-dinh-Diem and his brother advisor Ngo-dinh-Nhu, and then translate it into English for future use by USAID.

The CIA sponsored program of sending teams of saboteurs and spies into North Viet Nam using Nguyen-cao-

Ky and his flight crews with their C-47's had so frequent leaks that finally it was scrapped and they decided to bring the Taiwan C-46 crews in for those super secret missions. I was instructed to help them getting their plastic laminated Vietnamese ID cards. So I frequently went to their villa at 2-E Nguyen-thanh-Y street and work it out with their leader Col. Bob Yeh who also had his name changed to Diep-chan-Thanh. Every time they rotated their aircraft I was offered lots of fresh fruits from Taiwan, oranges, tangerines, pears and melons.

I also was given the task of reorganizing the Huynh-huu-Bac officers club. I then coordinated with base engineering to built a false ceiling equipped with light fixtures and speakers from above to give it a more cozy and warm atmosphere. And I recruited Mr. Nam Co to be in charge of the kitchen who owing to his skill and inventiveness had offered tasty meals at a very reasonable costs. The base engineering also built a huge dancing floor on the back yard of the club complete with lights under and around its perimeter. During each weekend and holiday there were dancing parties with the orchestra of Lieutenant Hoang-minh-Tuynh featuring all the famous songstresses of the time.

Around the end of 1960 there was a visit of a big delegation of the school of Salon de Provence flying into Tan-son-Nhut in several French transport planes. Then Colonel Vinh as an ancient Salonais asked me very nicely if I could help in their reception. I got the assistance of Mr. and Mrs. Cong-xuan-Bach the former owners of the notorious Phu-Gia French restaurant at the Hoan-Kiem lake in Ha-Noi catering a good dinner while with the help of the young Le-vinh-Hoa of Salon 54 we organized a big gala night. All the Saigon beauties escorted by Vietnamese officers in their all white uniforms danced and had fun till early next morning.

I remember that one day I took the initiative to put up a fashion show in concert with the fashion boutique La Maison Rouge in Eden Gallery. I had them build an elevated runway going from the back verandah of the club to the center of the dance floor with flood lights and public address apparatus. It had taken almost two month of preparation, selection of models and training them to walk to the tunes of music to show the dresses made by the fashion designer houses. We finally were able to get two models, the wife of captain Tran-minh-Thien and my wife under my very pressing supplications. Each lady presented four elegant dresses custom made by La Maison Rouge and was escorted to the stage by an elegant Major Nguyen-ngoc-Oanh, marching gingerly on the runway to the joyful music under a roaring applause from the audience. And the fun went on with an all night dancing.

I have to mention that one of my left hand jobs had been put to good use when both me and my wife went together with tape measures and pins to the American residences for making dresses to those ladies. One case of note was when we made an elegant dress in Thai silk for Mrs. Elliot the wife of Colonel George Elliot.

1962 started with the rumor that the American forces could join in the fight. While I was at my desk doing nothing that morning suddenly my telephone rang. At the other end an American voice said "may I have Captain Cung please?" I answered asking who is it and then the reply came in clear "I am Captain Beauford J Price your classmate at Squadron Officers School 59, do you remember me?". I said "of course how can I forget the buddy who took me to base hospital ER when I almost suffocated with an allergy attack, but where are you and how I can help you"? Beauford said that they were in their C-124 and about to land, bringing a mobile radar unit and having instruction to coordinate with me for a set up site. I rushed to the landing strip and guided them to an empty site behind the Liaison squadron.

Another day when I leisurely relaxed at home enjoying my Tet Holiday an US Army jeep pulled to a full stop and down came an Army Colonel introducing himself as Colonel Preiss of the USARIIS (United Army Riukiu Island Support). "I am sorry to disturb you for this Tet but I had order to coordinate with you for a location to set up our advance team due to land very soon".

I put on my uniform and rushed out in his jeep steering him to an empty location full of wild vegetation behind our Transport Group hangars. Their team had about 40 NCO's who put their hands to the work at once, clearing the spot, erecting their canvas tents, setting up desks using their military crates and installing their typewriters and communication equipments. In no time you started hearing the humming and clicking as they got busy working with their headquarters in Okinawa.

The next morning Colonel Preiss came to see me saying that according to their regulations his men must have frequent GI haircuts and wondered if I could give him some help. I took him to my barber shop in Lang-cha-Ca and got my preferred barber to come along with his tool box. Things seemed to have been taken care of when the colonel came again looking very embarrassed and telling me that the barber did a very nice job but he did not know anything about sanitation requirements and was unaware of what we wanted him to do. So I had to be at the site for nearly one hour trying to explain to him in simple words the sanitation requirements and what flat tops mean and look like.

One week later during one of our casual encounter Colonel Preiss suddenly said that barbering for the US forces is a very big business. When he was in India a local man had made a nice fortune just doing that and he wondered why I would not give it a try. I answered that being an officer in active duty I could not do it but if he could lend me a copy of his regulation on barbering services I'd show it to my wife and may be we could find a way.

A few days after Preiss took me and my wife to the Navy Exchange on Phan-dinh-Phung street to introduce us to Commander Kispert and after a short interview my wife signed a concession contract that lasted for almost ten years. We opened our first shop in Tan-son-Nhut and then after in MACV, Long-Binh, Vung-Tau spreading to Nha-Trang, Da-Nang. Phu-Bai, Chu-Lai, A-Shau, An-Khe,…and even during the VC Tet offensive teams of barbers with their toolkits had to wait in my house for the US jeeps to take them out to hot spots, at the artillery pieces or the front line perimeter defense sand bags.

We used equipment and beauty barbering supplies furnished by the Exchange services netting us about one million a month. All my young brothers pitched in to help managing and controlling. I was always kidding with my friends that I had turned my downfall into a glorious win-win situation with money flowing in like in a storm drain. But as they said "fortune coming from the sky would go back to the land", we had invested in modern pigs farms in Thu-Duc, in a 15,000 acre cattle ranch in Phan-Thiet and in several villas rented to Americans. All those had become "property of the people managed by the communist state".

In 1960 there was a coup attempt by the paratroopers on the 12th of November. While every one was trying to guess about the situation, I was relaxing at ease on my front porch when in the morning of the 14th a jeep driven by Nguyen-cao-Ky with Nguyen-chanh-Thi on the passenger side and two paratroopers armed to their teeth came to a sudden stop. Ky called me and asked for the key to the ammo storages so that they could take napalm bombs and drop to the Gia-Long palace ground from a C-47. I answered that I had no more control of anything and they should go to Nguyen-Trung-Son's house for that. And a moment later the coup completely failed Phan-Phung-Tien flew to Thailand with the whole leadership group and Nguyen-Cao-Ky stayed behind to lose his credibility from that day on.

As for me I gave a long sigh of relief since my wife being ready to give birth to our last son Tran-tuan-Tai we were very tense to figure the way to take her to the maternity ward (I took my wife to Hung-Vuong Hospital on the 16th and Tai was born on the 19th).

During that time I had sold my Citroen car because the maintenance and gas cost would be too prohibitive for my meager income. I had bought a more modest Velo Solex and during noon break I would gingerly go to a few foreigners' home for teaching, French to Mr. Farrolan the ambassador of the Philippines, Vietnamese to Mr. Dick Adams of USAID and adviser to the Minister of finance Nguyen-Luong and English to the former Captain Cottet presently with the aircraft sale company of R.J. Cross to supplement my humble captain salary. That is why my personal file with security would have listed me as not only a notorious Dai-Viet member but also a pro French, pro American and who knows what, maybe a CIA agent to complete the menu.

Also to have more income my wife had to work as medical visitor for the pharmaceutical firms of Dang-Quoc-Co and Chuong-van-Vinh. My boss Colonel Nguyen-xuan-Vinh had also the goodness to refer me to Lieutenant

Colonel Nguyen-van-Chau, the director of psychological warfare and a powerful protégé of president Diem to go to his home in Tan-Dinh every night and teach him English. Then when Chau was sent to attend the Community Development Conference in Baguio sponsored by Mr. Binamira, a rising star in the Philippines political scene and minister for community development I had the chance to join his delegation along with professor Vu-Quoc-Thong. I had become the spoke person for the Viet Nam delegation, joining several sub committees symposiums and going to the podium to read the Viet Nam delegation findings and motions.

Then on February of 1962 the renegades pilots Quoc and Cu dropped bombs on the Independence Palace. A few days before the happening I had Lieutenant Phan Ngo, an air force administration officer at my desk and leisurely talking about the political situation when he suddenly asked me on the possibility of a change. I answered that he should see it with the guys of the fighter outfit in Bien-Hoa. Right after the tense day of the Quoc-Cu rebellion all officers of VNAF headquarters along with units commanders had to wear their white uniforms and led by Nguyen-xuan-Vinh, they all went to Gia-Long palace to listen to President Diem's grievances.

All of us were lined up in full attention on a semi circle in front of the President, who, dressed in a white suit and displaying a ruddy face, gave a lengthy monotonous speech in a thick Hue accent, his eyes always looking down to the floor. My impression was that all of us had tensely got some words while missing others and there was a feeling of relief when we got out of the palace.

A few days later Vinh summoned me to his office and with a clearly satisfied expression on his face he told me to report immediately to Colonel Do-Mau the dreaded director of military security. Feeling a chill in my spine I stepped out looking for transportation when Lieutenant Nguyen-van-Huu passed by on his Vespa scooter asking whether I am going to the security office. And he told me to mount on his back seat and took me to the place. As I knew that Huu was a Dai-Viet member of the South branch and Quoc being a VNQDD while Cu was the son of Cu Luc a prominent VNQDD member, I smelled troubles. Huu dropped me off at 5 Binh-Khiem street and went on to another place.

Having the feeling of walking into a tiger den I gathered my strength and composure and went into Do-Mau office. There was an army captain, perhaps his aide, sitting behind a desk. When I saluted him he raised his stiff face and shouted at me: "how could you look so relaxed entering this place"? Boiling with anger I shouted back :"I am of equal rank, I saluted you first. Was the procedure here intimidation? If it was torture and beating I am ready!"

Then the huge dark hardwood door opened at a sudden and a face poked out, a sinister tanned face wearing dark sunglasses, hollow cheeks. Stretching his arms wide, Do-Mau whom I had never met before embraced me pulling me into his huge dark office with windows covered by heavy dark color drapes, a big stuffed tiger at the entrance, the whole office with only one desk lamp with green glass shade throwing a sinister green light all over. It was a very scary sight giving me a cold shudder along my spine. I stood there frozen and speechless not knowing what to do and say when he pushed me down onto a chair at the front of his enormous and massive desk. And he talked and talked in a low pitched voice about the dangerous VC insurgency. He said that if he still stayed at his present assignment it was for his love of the President but Mr. Ngo-dinh-Nhu was so sectarian.

Being aware of my activities in the past due to my ardent patriotism Do-Mau promised that from now on no one would follow me and he would sign now the paper promoting me to Major. With great relief I went back to my desk when I was again summoned to report to my superior at once.

There Colonel Vinh displaying a bumpy ruddy face with his blood injected eyes talked to me in his sarcastic voice: " Would you think that having Colonel Do-Mau's protection was good enough for you? If I pick this telephone up you will understand what I mean!" (it could be a special direct line to Mr. Nhu office). Fed up and disappointed I saluted and got out without saying a word.

During a staff meeting with all units commanders present Nguyen-cao-Ky of the Transport oufit suddenly took his pistol out of its holster and put it with a loud bang on the meeting table. Ky with his characteristic blunt and firm voice pointed his finger at Vinh saying "You might have good academics but your leadership was a big zilch. It is not admissible to bring politics into this air force. If people were assigned and promoted according to their allegiance to a party very soon you will see only incapables and valets around here". Vinh changed his complexion from a ruddy to a white ash pale color, turned his face down to the table without any other statement and the meeting came to an embarrassing end. There was rumor that Vinh will go to America for further training and it could be another case of "luring the tiger out of his laird", a clever and convenient way to dispose of an unwanted person whose credibility had become questionable.

Also during this period of time an event had occurred changing completely the turns of political and social happenings. While I was at my desk "picking my mustache and fly yawning" my telephone rang and there was a very heavy Southern voice saying " I am Colonel Pham-ngoc-Thao and I want Captain Tran-do-Cung". I replied "Yes sir, here I am but who are you and what can I do for you"? Then the same voice came back "I am Albert Pham-ngoc-Thuan, your classmate at Khai-Dinh, do you remember me?" I said "of course but I thought that you were district chief of Ben-Tre"? And Thao said "I have completed my job and now I work at the political advisor's office on Hong-thap-Tu boulevard. If you go up this way in the future please drop by and we can talk about our past souvenirs".

One day when I had something to do with the Central Purchasing Agency next door I decided to drop by, entering his place with much apprehension. After check and search by a soldier on duty I was led to his desk and I saw him, not much different from our time together in class 1-S more than two decades ago, still the same slender guy with same off tanned complexion and the same cross left eye. After about five minutes talking of our memories and before sending me off Thao vaguely wondered of how many of our classmates were still in Saigon and if we could get together some day there would be lot of fun just talking of our days together as school boarders.

On my way back I had the idea to have a get-together some times and thinking of our friend Pham-Quy, a prominent lawyer who had abilities to coordinate for a home dinner. I phoned Pham-Quy at once. Quy was also enthusiastic to get in touch with the few friends to come to his residence at 132 Cong-Ly for a dinner. That night we had a gathering of about ten persons including Commander Vo-Sum of the Navy, Ton-that-Uan director general of the Vietnam Power company, Doan-Hoa assistant director of the custom services, Tran-ngoc-Nhuy brother of Tran-ngoc-Lien the commissioner of agricultural credit, Ngoc-Tram well known as songstress Minh-Trang, Pham-ngoc-Thao and the Pham-Quy's we enjoyed an appetizing Hue dinner owing to the cooking and cleverness of Mrs. Pham-Quy.

The emotional conversations were all about souvenirs and memories of our young days, pure and innocent amid laughs with the promise to meet together at another time. A few months later, in about August Thao called me again and let me know that he now worked on his English at the Army language school to make ready for his training at the Leavenworth Command and staff school in America. He asked me to join him for lunch in the JGS compound but as I said I had no means of transportation he told me that he will come to pick me up.

At precisely noon time Thao came and I went in his Jeep to JGS thinking that we will go to the officers' club there. But to my surprise Thao turned left taking me to high ranking officers' compound and led me up stairs to an apartment next to the last one. He opened the door, ushered me in, and I met an Army Lieutenant Colonel who was introduced to me as Pham-dang-Tan, assistant to Colonel Do-Mau the Director of military security services. Tan then opened the fridge taking out to the table French bread and all kinds of cold cuts like ham, Italian sausage and liver pate and the three of us sat down to lunch.

Thao opened the conversation saying that the political situation was a disaster and changes were needed to remedy it. A coup was being ready with the support of most of the Generals, the one next door Khiem had given his OK as well as Colonel Do-Mau. The question now is when it started can you Cung take the air force into your hands. My answer was a clear no because the tradition in my air force is for a flyer to command it. Then they asked me whether I could suggest a name and after quickly reviewing the names that I know, I advanced the name Nguyen-cao-Ky who was dissatisfied at losing his commanding job of his transport group and will be transferred to Nha-Trang air training center.

But I cautioned that Ky was a cowboy ranger type, blunt talking, hot blooded, a kind of Tartarin of Tarascon. Tan, with his keen knowledge of all officers of the armed forces, gave a nod of approval. They then asked me to get in touch with Ky consequently. I said that as my relationship with Ky had not been very warm I'd try to do my best.

At home the next morning I took from my display case a bottle of Johnny Walker Black Label among the many bottles of liquor that my foreign students gave me, put it in a brown bag and went to Ky's office. I found him busy shuffling through the drawers of his desk to clean them out and make ready for the transfer to another guy. I saluted him, put the brown bag on his desk saying "I had so many good bottles of liquor as presents from my foreign students. But as I am not a connoisseur and seeing that you are about to change job I thought appropriate to offer this to you".

Ky heartily shook my hand clearly appreciative. When I went home during noon break and was about to sit down for lunch Ky suddenly stopped by and entered sitting down on my sofa. He said "I thank you for the gift but I am wondering why, is there anything behind"? I then told him in detail my meeting with Thao and Tan at Do-Mau's apartment and emphasized to him that it is a very confidential and dangerous situation and if he agrees I will let them know and they would coordinate directly with you. He then shook my hands and said yes.

According to the planned event when the coup started I along with Thao would be atop one separate armored vehicle heading to the Gia-Long Palace and I had to get in touch very often with him at his residence at 93 Tu-Duc Street to know exactly D day and H hour.

On the 28th of October I parked my car at a lot in front of the zoo and took a prepaid taxicab to go to Thao's place. When I pushed the bell button the guard soldier opened the square hole of the steel gate and talked in low voice "secret service". I looked back and saw across street three men in blue coveralls of the power company, busily working at an electrical concrete pole. I jumped into my awaiting taxicab rushing back to my parked car which was a brand new Morris 1100. I hurried back to the air base going through a couple of red lights and stayed put in there with the anxious thoughts that may be to night or the next one they will come for me, and I would not dare to exit the Phi-Long gate.

And that is why when the coup started the night of 31 October I did not participate in the operation atop an armored vehicle as planned. Instead I was at ease at my desk, my feet on it and listening to the news from a small radio.

It had been another case of mishap which turned out to be a lucky one because if I sat atop that tank I would not be sure to get out of it safe and sound. At about four a.m. Ky and his men came by dressed in their orange color flight suits with hardened faces smelling blood and armed to their teeth with hand grenades, sub machine guns and pistols dangling at their belt. Ky said to me "Cung you stay here taking care of the air force. We are going after Hien and then Sang". But he forgot about Mai, the air force Can-Lao rep and while Ky was busy running after the other guys Mai coolly called the Generals to report that "Things are normal at the air force, I am taking care of everything here and please Generals feel at ease".

And Mai naturally took the reins, kicking Ky aside. When Do-Mau sent to VNAF a paper promoting me exceptionally to full Colonel due to my participation in the uprising Mai showed it to me and said that he was asking for the air force to submit it for the sake of preserving the chain of command. And Mai was assigned as military attaché in Bonn and the matter was forgotten but I did not pull it out being only intent to get out of the services.

When we formed our tactical air wing 41 in Da-Nang Lieutenant Colonel Pham-long-Suu took me with him to be his deputy for materiel. But nearly two months later Nguyen-cao-Ky summoned me back to Saigon to help him prepare a briefing for McNamara on the planned VNAF development program. When that was done he retained me to be in charge of liaison with political parties.

Then I was given the responsibility to oversee the wedding of Ky with Tuyet-Mai at the big reception hall of Caravelle Hotel with a big attendance of high ranking dignitaries, Vietnamese , American and all the diplomatic corps, the cost being graciously covered by a special gift of Premier Huong. I'd like to elaborate a little bit on the romance Ky-Tuyet Mai. A few weeks after the 63 coup the Council of Generals decided to send out to Thailand the first good will mission represented by two young generals Nguyen-cao-Ky and Le-nguyen-Khang on our military C-47. Ky told me that day "as you had so close relationship with the leadership of Air Vietnam, maybe you can ask them to reappoint our airplane nicely for the trip"?

I called Nguyen-tan-Viet Director of Technical Services of Air Vietnam and with his approval our C-47 was towed to his shops. The work was beautifully done with wall covered by special commercial aircraft material and floor under special carpeting. Then airline reclining seats were installed with couch and meeting table and chairs. They also added a toilet facility and a mobile food warmer with a drink dispenser bar.

Ky liked it very much and the day before the departure he suddenly said that with such a beautiful surrounding it would be an eyesore if we could not have a nice female attendant on board. "Could you Cung arrange with Air Vietnam for that"? I gave then another call to Air Vietnam but this time I got the Director General Nguyen-tan-Trung who very quickly told me that they have a "Mai mot" meaning Mai number one who will be designated to go with the military party to Bangkok. And that was the story ending with courtship and romancing and the nice wedding reception at Caravelle Hotel. I had unintentionally become a de facto matchmaker.

VNAF Major, 07-62

My Family in Saigon, 1967

CHAPTER FIVE

V.- Farewell to Arms.

When Ky became minister of sports and youth of Tran-van-Huong's cabinet he gave me the position of Director of Cabinet. The military minister came only once with a helicopter landing on the yard in front of the ministry to the big applause of all employees, males and females. He also did not go to government meetings and I went in his place to witness the senility of prime minister Huong and vice premier Tony Oanh always busy filing his nails with detachment and lack of interest.

I also participated in the management of Air Vietnam with my recent assignment as member of its board of directors. Then the civil government of Dr. Phan-huy-Quat was in the making. Dr. Quat asked me to become his Secretary at the prime minister office. But as Dr. Hong would accept the post of secretary of sport and youth if he could retain me as his director of cabinet Dr. Quat gave that post to Bui-Diem.

I have to add that during that period of time all coups attempts had the involvements of Pham-ngoc-Thao and when the Lam-van-Phat coup failed Thao became the most wanted guy. He gave me, through a young girl messenger a short note asking my help by intervening with Ky. But seeing that the civil government had been formed I did not do nothing to further spoil the stabilized situation. I knew at that time that Thao was hiding above the ceiling of the

Emile Bodin sports store but the agents of Loan could not find it out and he finally found his way to the catholic area of Ho-Nai to be wounded, arrested and tortured to death.

When Dr. Quat relinquished his job after a bitter squabble with Chief of state Phan-khac-Suu the Generals pressed Ky to form his government. I was given the post of Commissioner General for Commodities distribution with the rank of secretary. During that time the VC mounted a vicious economic attack on the capital trying to choke the whole city to a complete panic. Pigs were not permitted to enter the capital creating shortage and price rises.

They also blocked the delivery of rice and for that they had the indirect collaboration of the Chinese merchants who had storage facilities in Binh-Dong and who took advantage of the situation to manipulate the market to their profit. Rice business had been for a long time under the control of the Cholon Chinese who had their own big storages, thrashing facilities and a complex system of loan sharking from the production to the distribution end. The price of rice kept going up day by day and when it reached 10,000. piasters for a 100kg sack of regular rice there was a real fear because the pay of an army captain would not be enough to buy three sacks.

There was another pressing problem, the shortage of individual transportation. The modest mopeds Mobilettes and Velo-Solex were under the sole distribution of the French company Denis Freres and they were not able to bring in enough to satisfy the demand. Besides according to the old definition of a French rule only bicycles with an auxiliary motor were permitted to be imported, blocking all others small motorbikes off the market. The city office was assigned the task of giving out coupons of mopeds to civil servants and military personnel who needed them. But the demand was so huge that the city was swamped and it created black market and corruption.

Roughly speaking the above are urgent things that I was facing with. Nevertheless my outfit was a new creation for the purpose of solving an urgent situation which was undermining the morale of the people and creating the distress of civil and military servants. And I had no office, no budget, no personnel, no defined job descriptions and no boundaries to my responsibility and prerogatives. I had to borrow the desk of Nguyen-van-Kieu (Nguen-van-Thieu's big brother) at the office of the APACL to temporarily set up my shop. And then the office of the Mayor decided to dump on me with relief all the files of applications for mopeds of the functionaries and military personnel. I had to call upon the help of the boy scout association to set up lottery and dispose of all pending cases as much as the supply on hand can satisfy.

I reported the situation to Premier Ky and he approved my plan composed of the following urgent actions: (1) to give us a loan of 500 millions from the National Bank to serve as operating budget, (2) to permit the importation of 19,000 Honda 50cc for the urgent need, (3) to authorize the import of 15,000 tons of frozen pork carcasses to be stored in a cold store to be built at the beer company as a safety level stock, (4) to build the Nguyen-Du supermarket as a model of modern marketing confronting the back door business dealing and black marketeering of Cholon. (5) to permit the seal off of the rice warehouses in Binh-Dong with military means for control.

Ky then convened a small meeting with me and Mayor Van-van-Cua at his desk and he said, half kidding and half serious, "I rely on you two for this pork business. If it could not be done satisfactorily I'd put both you in the freezer of BGI". Moreover I had to move head on against the resistance from the Ministry of Economy of Au-truong-Thanh, a sympathizer with the FLSVN (front of liberation of South Vietnam).

His department having traditionally the prerogative to give import and export licenses looked at my organization as an infringement to their authority and interest and therefore spreading the false rumor that I had a huge cut of commission for the Hondas and the frozen pork. But in fact they sent their man Lam-vo-Hoang to my office to write the import licenses. During one interview on TV when I was asked on my economic concept I gave back a barbed answer that my economic is a down to earth rice and meat thing completely different from the theory formulated by the high degree economists.

Au-truong-Thanh very eagerly pressed premier Ky to put my organization under his ministry but when he did not succeed he assigned his men to work under me pretending to help me out with good and capable employees, Le-phuoc-Trong as my deputy and Lam-vo-Hoang as my director of business, both men being either VC affiliates or sympathizers. In the mean time Nguyen-Du supermarket was completed and open to the public. It was an amazing success paving the ways to a string of small superettes everywhere.

I was invited by FMI (food marketing institute) to a symposium in Bangkok to give my input and experience on the import of super marketing concepts to Saigon. I felt so proud to know that while Bangkok was still hesitating we in Saigon had made our steps forward.

In May 1967 I was invited by the Trade Minister of Korea to a visit. May be when they saw me importing such a big number of Honda C-50 from Japan they would expect to get some business. That is why they welcomed me as a special VIP guest, took me to an inspection tour of their factory assembling motorbikes with parts imported from Japan, sightseeing their famous sites, treating me at those Ki-Shiang Houses and at night back to my hotel room there always was a nice girl awaiting to give me massage and other services. But due to my stressful work at home I got asthma attacks so often that I was unable to enjoy the third pleasure of men.

And then Honda invited me to stop by Tokyo and stayed there for three days being entertained by Mr. Soshiro Honda who took me out to visit his Honda Research and Development Center and test drive with him his Formula One which was the first car under development by Honda. When I bid farewell to him he gave a present for my wife which was a beautiful pearl necklace.

As for frozen pork, Company Van-Y which I did not know was the importer under license approved by the Ministry of Economy and the meat provenance was fully unknown. The only award to me was when the cold storage ship stop at the Navy berth and all the meat was unloaded into the freezer of BGI and then some got to the market the price of pork went down gradually to an enthusiastic welcome of the inhabitants of Saigon.

Afterwards when I was given the opportunity to visit the gigantic slaughterhouse in Buenos Aires, Argentina then I was aware that the pigs were from communist Tchecoslovakia , slaughtered in Argentina and sold to us anti communist guys through the intermediary of the Jews. What a tortuous arrangement where the dollars are almighty, above any beliefs and political structures!

That was why on my return I was invited to stop over in Tel Aviv where a Jewish Major armed with submachine gun took me and my wife to Jerusalem across a battle field still junked with all kinds of burned out Russian tanks during the recent Six Day War with the Egyptians. During this short trip we had the opportunity to visit the road of sufferings traveled by Jesus Christ under his cross, the famous wailing wall and also the sacred stone where he was laid on.

Speaking about stress, I was sure it was in my innate character always meeting head on with any obstacles. And there were so many of them, the VC or the Chinese mafia which sent me death threat messages, the pressing demands from the population for immediate results, the confrontation with the mafia at the department of economy and the rift between Ky and Thieu who labeled me Ky's henchman.

To de-stress when I was approached by the young movie director Le-hoang-Hoa I accepted to be his guest star in a couple of his films, the first one produced by the movie and TV directorate titled 11.30 p.m. as a treating doctor at the ER after a vicious sabotage attack by a VC bomb squad, acting with veteran Doan-chau-Mau, and the second one titled "Purple Horizon" as an armored Colonel produced by the firm My-Van Films acting with Mong-Tuyen, Kim-Vui and Hung-Cuong. During a cabinet meeting one secretary had voiced his concern about his colleague acting in movies. My reply was quick and blunt. "So what? Did I steal?".

At the end of 1967 I left the Commodities supply office and was replaced by Trinh-hoanh-Mo and then went on to the National Center for Rehabilitation to become assistant to Dr. Nguyen-huu-Vi. In January 1969 I was transferred back to VNAF where General Tran-van-Minh nicely told me to stay on working with old friends pending my next promotion to a higher rank. But secretly my only desire was to get out of the military services, my left hand business with barbering services to the GI's was in full swing, each and every month all expenses deducted we still netted in the millions.

Nevertheless just about two months later I was summoned by the ministry of defense to take the management and organization of the Asian Pacific Anti Communist League Conference. I set up my office at Majestic Hotel and worked there for a few months with personnel recruited from various public and private enterprises.

Then came the Asian Parliament Union Conference for our Assembly of Representatives, and the South East Asia Conference on Family Planning for the Department of Health. I went with Commander Vo-Sum of the Navy to Phnom Penh to help them set up their APACL Conference there and realized that the Khmers had a much better conference facility than ours at Majestic Hotel.

During that conference by a motion introduced by the Chinese Delegation we had been nominated as special advisors to APACL. Came the International Conference on Asian Development to be staged by the Ministry of Planning and Development and I was also given that work so that I spent more than one year at my Majestic Hotel office.

Afterwards Dr. Le-tuan-Anh Minister of Planning and Development requested the Ministry of Defense to assign me permanently to his department to be in charge of the feasibility study on the establishment of the future export processing zones in Long-Binh and Tan-Thuan-Dong. I was sent abroad to Ma-San in South Korea and Kao-Shiung in Taiwan for a few weeks to see on the spots the management and operation of their successful EPZ's. As foreseen, I received the retirement paper due to attained age on 31st of

March, 1974 with a retirement pay of 96,271. piasters every quarter which, translated into dollars on the black market at that time would give me $15. a month. I got my first two payments and then I left everything behind for a still uncertain future in America.

I decided to drop everything off thinking that I had given most of my productive life to the service of my country, five years as a contractual civil servant in the government and more than twenty years with the armed forces. Then I am free to do everything for me and my interest. I can now be directly involved in the operation of our chain of barber shops under concession with the Post Exchange or go very often to Binh-Thuan to oversee the deep well drilling in search of water for the need of our herd of 500 local cows to be artificially inseminated with frozen Simmental sperms imported from America, by my colleague Robert Saxton.

In October of 1974 I was given a scholarship from the FAO to go to the University of Los Banos in the Philippines for a three months training on Dairy techniques and Husbandry under the Danes with Dr. Stobberup and his team in the Faculty of Dairy Husbandry and Processing. I stayed on campus and the class had fifteen students from India, the Philippines, Ceylon and Thailand, mostly veterinarian Doctors.

I was graduated top of the class, specially distinguished in microbiology and dairy lab testing. The UP campus is located about five miles from the small town of Los Banos and I often took a ride in the colorful jeepsters to visit the place and get a first hand knowledge of their people.

One time I had problems with my wisdom tooth and went for treatment in a local dental office. The female doctor said that the tooth grew sideway and pushed on the other molar and offered to remove it. I asked about the other three and she said they did not have any problem now but in the future they might too. Then I asked her whether she could remove all four and she said yes if I could stand it. And things were quickly done with not too much discomfort but the Doctor recommended me to walk back to the school instead of taking the jeepster and if at night there would be too much bleeding I should use ice cubes on the wounds but to my amazement I had no problems at all.

I also took regular busses to Manila and on one occasion I visited Dr. Buu-Hoan at the Asian Development Bank to brief him on my dairy and cattle ranch at home for a possible loan in the future. Back in Saigon there were a number of bids offers for the supply of medicinal drugs and dehydrated rice to ARVN by the Americans under the Vietnamization program. With my connections I became the middleman for the two big firms of Tenamid and OPV and they gave me a cut of a few millions piasters.

CHAPTER SIX

VI.- Looking For The Way Out

The military situation was very alarming. The people worried very much specially when the press reported on the many battle losses and withdrawals. Our oldest son Tuan-Anh had got his permit visa to go to America for study but still wanted to stay on a few days to enjoy our traditional Tet with the family. We had to rush him out and we sent him off at the end of January 74 having so just one less thing to worry about.

Then we lost Banmethuot, retreated from the high lands and Da-Nang and the whole I corps were under heavy pressure. The population very hurriedly left their homes. And our devoted chauffeur Nham being a Southerner and having his wife in the country side was knowledgeable of the real situation always urged me "Colonel please find the way to take the whole family out, you won't be able to stay here!".

I then went to the Navy place and was told that in case of necessity I might come there. But seeing that there would not be much chance since the Navy family members were so many and then during a dangerous situation how could we go through all the obstacles on the way.

Very luckily one of our renters Mr. William Pittman having a Vietnamese wife told me one day that he knew one flight crew who would help illegally take our families out but without any male members. So on that morning of the 15th of April one USAF van backed into my house gate and took my wife and my kids out to where a C-130 sat ready to take off. While I was awaiting for the news at around seven that night my telephone rang and at the other end Mr. Pitmann voice said "happy landing". Giving out a big sigh of relief but in thinking of my fate it would still be subjected to an unknown star.

A few days later Dao Manh Tu and N.T. Thao formerly working under me but now with PANAM showed up with an Air Vietnam male flight attendant and we sat down in my flower garden at the front of my house. They said that all the VNAF top brasses had already their planes at the ready to take off. The mechanics were working hard on those airplanes but knowing that they would not be permitted to go along they planned to hijack those and with the ready help of some flight crews they would make their way out if I accepted to lead them. I answered that "I would stay out of the plan and you boys could do what you would see suitable".

The next day I went to Vung-Tau with chauffeur Nham looking for the possibility to hire boats to go out to sea where the 7th fleet was, but things looked very difficult and besides, you would not know anyone whom you could believe and rely on. Back home one very remote acquaintance Mr. Vinh-Thanh the owner of the Duy-Tan hotel in Dalat where I attended the economic conference came and stayed in my place thinking that I might be his chance. On the day of 20th of April he got a connection with an American who promised to take us out at $400. each to be paid in advance. Having $800 in my pocket I paid him right away with the condition to be fully refunded if we could not go as promised.

Then I contacted General Vo-Dinh of VNAF who graciously let me use his half finished villa at the officers new housing area of Tan-son-Nhut as a staging place. We were about twenty persons that night, including the family of Trinh-vinh-Dien of Shell Oil fighting off all the swarms of blood hungry mosquitoes. But in the morning the scheme failed and I was repaid fully as promised. Vinh-Thanh told me that he owned a villa in Monterey and when we would be there he would open a restaurant for me to work at the front with customers while he would be in the back with the kitchen. In despair and close to your death it would be a beautiful and comforting dream.

When I went to DAO at their former bowling area I saw a big crowd squatting or lying down everywhere among them there were a few VNAF officers who at seeing me turned their face away with furtive eyes. On the roadway to Tan-son-Nhut airport a flock of people kept moving on with suitcases and packages giving me a more pressing urgency and despair. I decided to go to the headquarters of VNAF, but in there I encountered a luke warm atmosphere and Do-van-Ry the general's aide turned his face down to his papers ignoring my presence, totally different than when he came to my office seeking a permit to buy a C-50 bike.

On the 26th while I moved around aimlessly in my LaDalat car feeling as a fish in a jar or a bird in his cage suddenly a white Toyota driven by an American stopped waiving at me. He then shouted "why you are still here at this moment?" He was Cal Thimsen the vice president of computer science corporation and a good friend having a share in my cattle venture. I told him that I am still looking for a way out and he said "come to my house tonight". He told me later that the US government now authorized American companies to take their employees out and during the last few days he kept bringing his Vietnamese wife family members to the airplanes.

He asked me to let him use one of my villas as a staging place. So I joined in as his employee and was able to get Mme Hong with her two kids Hien and Uyen going along. There were about twenty people gathered for a military flatbed to take all of us to BOQ-1 awaiting for the next flight.

We were all sleeping on the bare floor and Thimpsen provided us with food from the military canteen. For two days there was no bus because the Vietnamese drivers went on strike. Finally an American had to drive the bus to take us to check in and boarding on the last flight out on an USAF C-130, the afternoon of the 27th of April just before the bombardment of Tan-son-Nhut.

A real near miss, on board there was a big crowd sitting on the bare floor, some sobbing, others crying tears coming down cheeks and the majority doom and gloom, tired faces, speechless, staring at no where may be still numb with such an ordeal they have been through.

When the aircraft was in the international airspace I opened my briefcase taking out a bottle of champagne and uncorked it with a mute bang. Then I passed it around for each one to have a sip to our evasion and our freedom. We landed in Guam at eleven p.m. and were greeted by the volunteer ladies of the Red Cross offering to each of us a cup of hot chicken broth.

Guam just got order to receive refugees that was why they just started leveling the land to erect tents but they did not yet have time to provide bedding and a minimum of toilet facilities. When the busses took us to our assigned tents it was not a real shock for me being used in the past to my boy scout life. But for others it would appear as a heart breaking disaster, such a sudden tragic downfall. I got Hien with me to the central supply place to get mattresses, blankets and those miscellaneous things like toilet soap tooth brushes and pastes and haul them back to our tent to set up for the night.

Outside in the dark night engineering equipments still digging trenches for latrines and running plumbing pipes to the temporary washing facilities as well as stringing electrical wiring for lights. Very early in the morning I went out and saw that the tent city was already full of so many people and there were tents over tents and groups here and there talking in bewilderment.

I started to see some of the familiar faces of the past elegant Saigon but now every one was just alike very equal, their heart saddened by the big loss and very worrisome of the uncertain future. I went to the information center for news and to broadcast the search for my family. I came across with my best friends Mr. and Mrs. Vu-ngoc-Tuyen sitting out there looking wilted and very sad, a white wet washcloth on their head as a barrier against the harsh morning sun of Guam. When they started registering names for America I signed on for Camp Pendleton thinking that my family should be there already with our son in Monterey. But on 5 May when we took off, the plane changed course to Fort Chaffee, Arkansas because there was news that the local population was demonstrating against the coming of refugees from Vietnam.

Fort Chaffee was an old army base and had good facilities. Each family was assigned enough rooms with good toilets and showers providing adequate comfort for a stay until sponsored to go out. Around those quarters the streets had sidewalks with a few small PX stores selling things that you might need and even ice cream and goodies such as candies and cookies.

The refugees were feeling more easy and they went out, well dressed going along the sidewalks, chatting or greeting each other, exchanging news and rumors just like along the Tu-Do street before. I once more went to the information office for another broadcast searching for my family.

Before leaving Saigon my mother gave me eight ounces of gold as a safe guard. I went to a Jewish store and sold them for $2,300. and felt more secure with cash in my pocket. A few days later I haphazardly came across with a group of five VNAF generals with general Nguyen-van-Manh of the JGS who just came in. After hand shaking I asked them: " What are you going to do now"? General Minh of VNAF then very simplistically said "We are not going to worry because the Americans will take us to the Pentagon for a debriefing and get first hand experiences on the war".

How naïve they were! Then I said "I could not have anything in that business" and I shook their hands good bye. In the vast compound they had set up four or five mess halls to cater to such a huge refugee population. Everyday I went to another mess hall with the hope to find my folks there.

Then one day as I went to a remote site and stood in line there suddenly I saw at the far end of the hall in one of the many chow lines my wife and my kids filing through. I hurriedly left my place, went around to the other line and very discreetly approached my wife in her back wrapping my arms around her, blindfolding her with my two hands. It was a strong emotional time, all my kids speechless with teary eyes, my wife sobbing, crying and kissing, mumbling thanks to Buddha and God.

She told me that everywhere she went during the odyssey she kept going out at night to kneel down and pray for her husband escape to safety. I went to the office and requested that we be relocated to the same place and then along with Hien, Uyen and Vinh we moved to Bao's apartment where we shared bunk beds and opened our hearts recounting the so many events that had happened during just a few short weeks. Then Uyen and Chau would go out day in day out buying ice cream and roasted chicken legs for the whole group to enjoy.

Everyday I paid visit to the central office of the camp and the various volunteer agencies for pertinent useful information. From time to time they broadcast news of an approaching twister and we had to rush back to safety. I met quite a few old friends and we talk sharing personal experiences of our evasion to safety, each and every one with his own special circumstances and lucks.

I attended a meeting where we were briefed on life in America and the story of the founding of America with the coming of refugees from all places on earth. There was one thing that I considered very crucial that was" to try to go to mainstream America and avoid grouping together ghetto like".

One day the owner of a dairy ranch in Arkansas came looking for me because he knew that I had been trained by the Danes. He offered me to be the assistant manager of his ranch to become full time manager when his son will leave with a proposed starting salary of $800. With such an attractive starting pay and seeing that the job offered is fitting to my background I requested him to give me a proposed contract so that I could discuss with my wife. She thought that it would be a demanding and tough job but to get ready for it she went to the clothing distribution center and picked up a few sturdy blue jeans that would be suitable for farm work.

On the same day I got a telephone call from the Lutheran Refugee Service telling that a Monterey Lutheran Church offered to sponsor our family. Thinking of our oldest son Tuan-Anh being a student at the Monterey Peninsula Community College we thought that the better move would be a complete family reunion first. Then I told the Arkansan rancher that I would have to get my family together in Monterey and then I'd be back working for him.

CHAPTER SEVEN

VII.- Building Freedom

On the 3rd of July we left Fort Chaffee, changed flight at the colossal Dallas airport and landed at Monterey airport at almost noon time. One delegation of the church greeted us at the airport, embraced and kissed each one of us warmly and sincerely. We remember that there were Pastor Lineberger and his wife Sarah, Mr. and Mrs. Hal and Larene Kauffman, Mr. and Mrs Ed and Karen Barker. We were escorted to our address at No 6 of 9th street which the church had rented for us with all the needed furnishings with TV and fridge. We specially appreciated their detailed care by making available to us chopsticks and bowls, rice and even a bottle of fish sauce in the fridge. We occupy the apartment down stairs and up stairs was Navy Captain Muoi big family.

I was told that this church sponsored only three families of high ranking officers of the Army, Navy and Air Force and their board had mostly retired officers of the US Navy. Pastor Lineberger was a retired Navy captain and many of them were from families uprooted from their communist countries. That is why they treated us as their own relatives and we had the comforting feeling of being their long lost brothers.

The next night we went to the hill of the Presidio to watch the 4th of July fireworks, each one of us was given wool blankets being exposed for the first time to the cold foggy weather of Monterey. Almost frozen and shivering we watch with awe and amazement the splendor of the fireworks marking for us an advance taste and the significance of the Independence Celebration of this country which we felt now as our new adopted country. Each day the church ladies took turns taking us to markets for groceries. Then they gave us the orientation on job seeking.

Pastor Lineberger personally helped me type jobs applications listing my appropriate experiences and backgrounds accordingly and he took me to the contemplated places for interviews. I finally was accepted by J.C.Penney. When I saw the manager Kirk Hiassen he expressed doubts whether I could fit in with the shoe department which was short of hands. I then said “please let me try without pay and decide afterward”. Smiling he told me that “we have to pay if you work here” and assigned me under Gail Cantrell the department manager with 25 years of experience and having such a difficult character that for long he was looking for an assistant and no one would stick with him.

During my first 16 hours of training I had to learn technical things of shoes, the names, models, their stock numbers and related location in the warehouse. About two weeks later I had become fully knowledgeable of most things and therefore was given 40 hours per week at $2.65/hr and Cantrell left me alone to oversee the entire department. I had the reputation of making often multiple sales and one day a very pleasant thing happened. That morning Gail was with a tall customer and I did not know what he did or how he behave that the man went to see Mr. Hiassen complaining “You better let Cantrell go and give his job to that Oriental man”.

At work here I had a pleasant encounter. One late June evening one Oriental lady came in with her two kids to buy shoes for their back to school. I took their feet measurements and was showing them different shoes styles when suddenly I heard the lady use one Vietnamese like interjection with the little girl. I was not quite sure and asked "Are you Chinese or Vietnamese"? When she gave me her positive answer we started chatting a little bit in our native tongue and then I asked for her husband's name. She said Vy, Nguyen Quy.

I remembered having known Vy in Hanoi a long time ago in 1946 and when Vy came in from a tobacco store across street he recognized me and we also knew that Vy was related to my wife as close cousin. Vy had taught Vietnamese at the Defense Language Institute for a long time.

My daughter Minh-Chau did her kitchen cleaning at the Butcher Shop, a fine restaurant in Carmel, Thanh-Huong was a seamstress for a jacket factory, Tuan-Anh took care of the residence of a wealthy family in Pebble Beach, Tuan-Tai did odd jobs in the neighborhood. My wife also had a job in a tailor shop, sobbing while working wondering why she was being downgraded so tragically. I always consoled her and did not let her know that although every day I went to work with jacket and tie as neat and imposing as in Vietnam before, my job was not that all beautiful, also sweeping and cleaning, hauling and moving heavy boxes.

As for my kids they seemed very eager and pleased maybe because for the first time they were able to make money helping the family. All the paychecks were given to daddy. That was why when the house of 9th street were sold and we moved to 37 Ralston Drive and the church offered to pay the rent we refused the offer saying that we now had enough revenue for that.

Pastor Lineberger advised us against welfare and we only applied for food stamps and got $250. in coupons, a rather big sum of money for a family of six because we only bought essential staples like fish, meat, rice, bread, milk, vegetables and fruits.

Each month on exactly the first I went to Greg Shankle Real Estate to pay our rent in cash. One day while I was waiting for Mrs. Shankle to write a receipt Mr. Shankle came in, his wife called him and introduced me: "this is Bob Tran". Greg warmly shook my hand and said: "I heard many good things about you at J.C.Penney, My mother-in-law happened to be a sales clerk there for quite a long time. Why don't we go upstairs for a cup of coffee"? After chatting for a while with Greg on many things specially my academic background and my past experiences in Saigon, Greg said " now I know more about you and with your abilities and know ledges this country should be a land of opportunity for you. You should go into business because with J.C. Penney it would only be penny money." I said I did not have any money and did not know nothing about business here.

Greg looked up through his window and said across street they were building a 7-Eleven store and advertised for a franchisee on the billboard. He explained to me the 7-Eleven and franchise system and said if I wanted he would contact them for me. Seeing that there was nothing to lose I agreed and shook his hand.

One week later I had the visit of Miss Kathy Letterman, the company field representative. She stayed with me for quite a while telling me about the system and the money requirement for investor, I told her that I did not have any money and did not know anything of the business here.

Kathy then said she was only doing her job and promised to come once more next week.

I had become more assertive this time because the church had been told by its New York Office that they might give a $3,000. loan without interest from their refugee enrichment fund. And then our second daughter Bich-Thuy, presently a student in France, informed us that she was making a transfer of $7,000. to us as seed capital. I gave to Kathy the good news but she said that I was competing with fourteen other applicants. I said then it would not be to my advantage competing with those local persons having ready capital and being more understanding of business. But Kathy just calmly gave me necessary papers to sign and went on explaining about the system, hours of operation etc., and added like before that she was just doing her job.

In the mean time I went on with my shoes sale job with very good results and one day Mr. Hiassen invited me out for a cup of coffee. Being entertained by the big boss was felt as a high honor but there were no indications of what will happen, award or penalty or pay raise? In a very nice restaurant on Alvarado street, after a few chats of routine character the boss said that I had shown my outstanding ability and now was the appropriate time to offer me a department manager position. If I approved he would let Chicago know so that they could proceed with a training program. I will get weekly instead of hourly pay and the starting salary would be $275./week.

It was felt as a surprise jump and I agreed immediately. The next day a personnel representative from Chicago came with paperwork completed and from then on I had a separate desk with my own telephone. I was rotated for training in different departments, ladies, men, cosmetics, jewelry, toys, etc.. In the morning I had to come early with all department chiefs to provide cash to registers, check the displays and verify the general cleanliness of the whole store before opening the door for customers.

The work was pleasant, salary fair with full benefits there was nothing more for me to expect and may be I'll stay here until retirement. But from time to time I still remembered Shankle's words "you have to remember Penney money is penny money". America is the land of opportunity for everyone, those who came first and those who came later, providing that you were always positive and not being afraid of hard work and difficulties.

The Vietnamese had the advantage of being appreciative of the value of money liking to save instead of spending at will on the nonessential and superficial things. That is why the promotional business slogan of "spend and save" is not as appropriate as "do not spend and save".

I have opened an account at Wells Fargo and all the weekly paychecks were deposited in, the main disbursements would be for the rent, as for the food expenses they were covered by food stamps. I had saved enough to buy a new Toyota of the previous year model, the fifth car in my life. And from now on we do not have to wait for the transit busses and everyone of us could be ferried to work or to school with ease.

Life was easy and stable and I completely forgot about my investment in a Seven Eleven store. Then one nice and sunny Fall Friday while I was doing some paper work at my desk my telephone rang. From the other end an American polite and relaxed voice said "I am Bill Ososki 7-Eleven district manager in Aptos. Could I see you and your wife this noon in Aptos". I said it was impossible because on

Friday the store will close at 9 p.m. and then I'd have to check all revenues and take to the drop chutes at the bank.

His reply was "I'd see about it and I will get back to you later". At 2 p.m. Ososki called back saying "how about at 11 p.m. to night". I said yes, overexcited, may be had Heaven opened the door for me?

Back home we took a quick bite and went out early because I had to probe my way. When we arrived at the address it was still too early and we had to enter a next door ice cream parlor enjoying our ice cream and reading the newspaper.

At five minutes before time we went in and knocked at the door and were met by a group of five persons. Kathy Letterman, whom we had known, and we were introduced to Bill Ososki district manager, Pat Lawson, his deputy and two other persons who were administrative and finance managers. They steered us into their meeting room and after their detailed questions I said "as Kathy had been informed we do not have the initial $10,000. investment now. It was just a promise of loan from the church and the transfer of funds from my daughter in France as indicated from her letter and according to the requirement that money would be needed when we sign the contract".

Then Bill Ososki said "we must go next door for a private meeting". Five minutes later they came back and Ososki shook my hand saying "Mr. Tran you've got it" and he showed me the approval letter from the Region Manager waiving the payment of money until the completion of our training. I was bewildered and deeply moved when Mr. Ososki said "could you come back here tomorrow"?

When we were back the next day on a beautiful and warm morning we signed the franchise contract and were given the training program composed of one week of in store training in Sunnyvale under the supervision of Mr. Bob Barr and then a ten day classroom training in San Diego. I signed for our air tickets, the per diem money and the addresses of reserved motels at both places. On Monday going to work as usual I gave my resignation to Hiassen and he wondered if anything was unsatisfactory. Then I told him of my franchising of a 7-Eleven store to that he said it was a good move but if things would not be as I wished J.C. Penney would be pleased to welcome me back because my future here would be of a store manager position like him.

About our store training in Sunnyvale, the first thing we heard from Bob Barr was :" There is no free lunch in life. If some one gives you something he would expect to get something back from you." We were taught how to sell, how to deal with customers courteously and friendly, the technique of merchandising, how to take inventory, the relationship with vendors. And we were scheduled to work day, swing and night shifts. Bob Barr was an outstanding instructor and he made us feeling relaxed giving us confidence and trust. After the hands on week at the training store we were given one week break before flying to San Diego for the formal ten days classroom training.

During the break period we completed the paperwork for the purchase of our first home here. It was a good story. When Pastor Lineberger drove me out every day to job interviews we passed by a site close to 9th street where they were building a branch of Monterey Savings and Loan. I told him that our youngest son Tuan-Tai had $100. cash in his pocket which was his saving from years of selling bottles and old newspapers in Saigon. When this branch opened for business if Tai could become the first depositor it would bring good luck to him. Then Pastor got in touch at once with the board of directors of the bank and the next day along with Tai we were invited to the main bank on Alvarado street to see the Vice-President Bob Littlefield, the son of the President Mrs. Mary Mitchell.

After a long talk we were referred to his public relations officer who happened to have been helicopter pilot in Vung-Tau. He made the inauguration program and wrote the story for the Monterey Peninsula Herald. On that memorable day the bank gave Tai one hundred silver dollars in a cloth bag for Tai to carry on his shoulder and go to the cashier window, right after ribbon cutting, to deposit like in the scene of gold miners in the past. The moving scene was witnessed by the financial figures of Monterey and the Admiral commanding the Navy Post Graduate School.

When I got my franchise contract with 7-Eleven I thought of buying a house for tax advantage in the future, I then asked Greg Shankle for help and he brought us to a house in 2 Athens Court, Seaside. The house was perfect for the size of our family. Besides it was very close to my store, the price seemed right and we vouched for it. Then Greg said now is money matter, we need $8,000. down payment and a loan of $30,000. to wrap it up. I asked him the source of the loan and when he said Monterey Savings I asked him to give Bob Littlefield a call.

The following day Mr. Littlefield received me in his office and when I explained to him that for the down payment I'd need a little time to make arrangements because we had given to our son Tuan-Anh $10,000. when he came here for school in January 75. He then took me downstairs and introduced me to Mr. Ferrer the loan officer telling him "please do the impossible to give Mr. Tran this loan". Things were done quickly and on the loan document there was the annotation "credit investigation waived".

On the day we moved in our new residence we took off for San-Diego to continue our training. It was a near perfect organization. As soon as we landed one member of the training center was there to take us to the reserved hotel and give us the training program for the next ten days. Every morning a car picked us up and took us to the center.

The classroom was large and well equipped with desks and chairs and all the modern training aids, the teachers were young and highly capable. They taught us accounting, the management technique, the retail accounting method, the selection and interview of personnel, the periodic inventory taking, the estimate of loss and shortage by the use of red flags, the security and robbery prevention, and the understanding and use of the balance sheets. I had the feeling to be back to my former Squadron Officers School.

We were given tests every day and rated on our progress. During the training I got a call from Pastor Lineberger informing that the church had received the $3,000. from New York and they will send a check down. But I advised him to send it to the district office in Aptos instead. At the end of the training we received certificates of completion during one big reception with all trainees and teachers.

During our flight back we had a stop over for a couple days to visit the family of brother number 8 who was settled in Glendale after getting out of Camp Pendleton. After we reached home the bank informed us they have received $7,000. from France and I mailed a check to Aptos completing our commitment and everything fell into place as if some hand from up high was helping us.

But the store was not yet fully stocked and Kathy had to be there for a few weeks awaiting for the delivery and she had hired two local helpers so that all shelves be stocked up to standard. Then a Grand Opening was organized with banners showing 5 cent hot dogs, 5 cent money orders and free coffee in the presence of the Mayor of Seaside. The whole district was there giving us a hand while we were still timid.

Our entire family worked in the store. I had hired a new graveyard man and devoted full time training him. The result was that I had worked 24/24 but though I did not sleep and eat much I had not felt too tired.

The first day sale was a mere $156. But gradually it went up winning the confidence and heart of the neighborhood. After the first two years we reached a yearly sale of nearly a million dollars with a gross profit of 40% netting me around 8% even though in personnel expenses we already counted salaries of our children who worked in the store and went to school.

That was why the store was paid off in three years and the District had offered me a new store being built in Salinas using the equity of Seaside meaning that we did not have to use our own cash. Each day I went to Bank of America next door and deposited the daily receipt. Walking to the Bank with the bag of money and softly chuckling I could not have believed that in less than one year after being out of Fort Chaffee we already swam in main stream America.

Being used to a military life before with all the operational stand bys, restrictions and strict discipline, every night I went to bed keeping my blue jeans on and on my night stand was a telephone next to one tools box with hammer, hack saw, pliers, plumber and electrical tapes etc, so that in case of emergency I could slip on my shoes and be there in no time. I remembered one time my telephone rang and the night clerk told me that some body had driven on the landscaped area and broke a plumbing pipe sending water up like in a geyser. Seeing that it would not be any running water in store, meaning that in the morning there will be no coffee for early customers and then I would not get any plumbers at this late hour, I rushed out for any quick fix. I saw off a length of broom handle and tried to plug up the T joint. Under the thick fog and being doused with water I hammered the make shift plug in with all my force and finally the squirting out water was stopped.

My adrenaline ran high, I did not feel the cold and went in for a hot cup of chocolate before going home for some more sleep until the alarm clock got me up at 6 to go for closing the day business at 7 and proceed with shift transfer. On another instance I went out after midnight to relieve a sick clerk. There was no traffic after the beer and wine doors were locked and I went out working on the floor, mopping, cleaning and rearranging the shelves to their nice appearance when the door chime sounded. I rushed to the counter to see a big black woman with a shotgun at her right side pointing to the floor, walking and mumbling to herself "my kids are hungry". Then with calm I told her that if you need a gallon of milk or a loaf of bread we have them here and please help yourself. But seeing that she kept walking back and forth mumbling the same words I went out picking up the bread and milk putting them in a big brown bag and handed it to her. When she got out I called and reported to police who told me they caught her down street still walking with her shotgun and mumbling the same. It had been a cold sweat thing marking my life as a retailer here.

But it was not all. One nice Saturday morning at 9 a.m. I drove to Wells Fargo down the street to put my bag of money in the drop chute. I parked my car obliquely, stepped down and opened the chute to throw my bag in when I heard a stampede and a voice saying "this is a hold-up" with a gun pointed at me. The black guy wearing sun glasses and a knitted skull cap grabbed the bag and ran away to the other direction. I was going to the next store for a phone to report to the police when the black cop car pulled up. I was taken to the department to look for suspects in five big albums with all kinds of criminals mug shots. When I was through with no results they thanked me and let me go.

Three days later they asked me to be there one more time, When entering I saw a well dressed black man sitting in the waiting room. The policeman took me into his office and explained that this time I will be in a room looking through a one way glass and try to pick up the suspect among a line up of six men. I went through my elimination process. I set aside the black man I saw sitting in the waiting room when I came in. So there was just five men left and who would be selected to be the top prize. I eliminated the three ugly men and was confronted with selecting one of the two left. Both looked handsome and were of the same build then I saw a slight difference: I picked up the one having square athletic shoulders, The police officer then shouted "That is him, we got the guy" and he shook my hand taking me to a next door desk and handed me my bag which had been slashed cut, all cash gone except for the stack of food stamps and checks.

During the court session his lawyer asked me to the witness stand and she said "you told that it was a P-38 but now it was a 22 caliber gun"? I calmly replied that during that short tense moment how could I know for sure which is what? Having 20 years of war service in my air force I can say that I knew well all kinds of guns, including even some artillery pieces. Then the Judge asked me if I could recognize the criminal sitting in front of me. I then pointed my finger at him and the case was done. My wife asked me "Why did you show to the court the criminal? He will take revenge in the future".

Another time, it was about 10 in the morning while I worked in the cold room and my wife just finished checking the vendor Place and Gera I heard a very loud noise while the whole store shook. Thinking of an earthquake I rushed out to witness a terrifying scene. The whole front shelf was pushed to the back while the Pepsi 2 liters display case was toppled with all bottles on the floor uncapped and squirting out en force and zigzagging like rockets. The whole front windows were broken completely and in store sat a big blue Cadillac like in the show room of a car dealership. Luckily there was no casualty. My wife just getting out of the place face all green of fear and the same was for the Place and Gera guy who just finished stocking the shelf.

The Police came right away and cordoned the store and a tow truck was in to extract the driver and pull the car out. It appeared he was a senior with an artificial leg and when he stepped on the brake his foot slipped and got caught between the two pedals and the car just flew up above the front walk through the window into the store.

I called Phil Strodder our new field rep who came in no time and hired two persons clearing the place. The shelves were pushed back to their normal position and merchandise was restocked. The store was reopened after three hours without front windows and doors. Customers came in force some due to curiosity, all the ladies of the neighborhood were there, some bringing flowers to my wife, others food dishes and a few embracing us crying and saying "please do not leave us". And on that day sales went up sky high!

In November 78 the District gave us the newly built store #20176 on 1305 North Main street in Salinas. We then sold our house which had appreciated quite well and put all profit down on a good side villa in Oaks Hill, between Seaside and Salinas. Every day I had to commute between two stores for about 50 miles. I changed the business closing time to 7 a.m. for Seaside and 8 a.m. for Salinas. It meant that I had to be in Seaside at 6, get all the money out of the safe and start checking and counting until 7 when the day was closed and I could then finalize with all money in a bag to be dropped at Wells Fargo at once. Then I could leisurely go to Salinas to do the same thing for the 8 o'clock closing but at here I was able to finish all paperwork and went back to Seaside to complete the paperwork there.

Afterwards I had hired a retired US Army Master Sergeant from Fort Ort Bob Hollifield who after a couple of months working as sales clerk in all three shifts was trained to become Seaside store manager. I also got my oldest son Tuan-Anh to be store manager for Salinas to relieve me some bit. I finally sold the Seaside store to Bob Hollifield after ten year ownership with a hefty good will and financed him.

It is worthy to mention that on the 20th of July 1980 we celebrated the wedding of Tuan-Anh with Le-Chi and in October of the same year it was the wedding of Bich-Thuy with Thanh-Tung in Canada. At both events Mr. and Mrs. Carl and Alta Elder drove down all the way from Oklahoma to attend the nuptials ceremonies at the Japanese Buddhist Temple of Seaside.

The Grand Opening of Salinas store was an outstanding show for the whole city. The District had hired a Hulk climbing on the roof top with a huge release of multicolored balloons. All the accesses to the store were completely jam packed, blocking all traffic and the first day sale was more than $1,000. Even though the store was located on a safe main tract I had been through three dangerous situations.

On the New Year eve of 1982 I was called to take over from a sick sales clerk. I was there at 2 a.m. and while at the cashier stand I checked the cash and put the excess 20 single dollar bills in drop envelope #40 the door chime sounded. Then a tall Chinese came in, went around to the cooler doors and on to the coffee bar behind me. I had not had the time to drop envelope 40 down the safe when the guy jumped to behind me and said "give all to me". I felt a pointed thing in my back and calmly opened the drawer for him to get everything plus the drop envelope. At that moment a car pulled up and he fled on foot to the North direction.

The police were called in and I gave complete description of the man saying that he spoke English with a Mexican accent. The case had not been solved and I was told that in Mexico there were plenty of Chinese and perhaps in this case the guy just dropped in for a quick cash before running back to Mexico.

Another happening was in the eve of 1992. Very early at 4 a.m. of New Year 93 I pulled up and parked on the side of the store. It rained hard and while still sitting in my car I saw a big black man crossing from the other side of the street to stop on the front walk of the store shaking the rain off his head. Saying to myself that it was a case of someone needing an early warm cup of coffee, I stepped out of the car locked the door and hurried out greeting him. Then at a sudden he jumped on me, got me down to the ground and though I fought back he was able to turn me flat face down and took my wallet to run off to a back alley. It still poured down hard, I was soaked wet and the clerk on duty could not have heard anything. I called the police and gave complete report then spent quite some time calling all my credit cards to report losses. I had only $20. in my wallet. In the morning when I went to DMV to report and get my temporary driver license I then realized that I was still lucky because if that big guy hit me I would have been knocked out and gravely hurt.

When my son quit to go to Oregon I was lucky to hire a good manager who had plenty of experience working for a long time with 7-Eleven as an auditor going around every month to check the inventory of franchised stores. After working for three years under me I sold the store and financed him.

Then I retired fully at the age of 75 with a social security payment to both of us amounting to more than $2,000. per month plus all our monthly IRA withdrawals. Compared to my former military retirement pay in Saigon, it showed a real improvement. And we celebrated the weddings for Thanh-Huong, Minh-Chau, Tuan-Tai, and as such completing our responsibility with our family. Then we fully enjoyed our time with all our grand kids, did gardening, wood working, the profession of my ancestors, and I also tried my hands at cooking western cuisine.

When I went to the Hanoi University I initially enrolled in the PCB class as a preparation for my medical career. But my dad said that I had to study something requiring less time so that I could help all my brothers and that was why I quit PCB for sciences study.

One day Minh Chau asked me if you had to do it again would you go on with medical study to become a medical doctor? I then said I would go to a culinary school to become a chef. I had to add that we had sponsored the children of my brothers Loc and Hoang, Huy-Tuan and Hoang-Huy, and when they came here we raised them like our own kids sent them to schools and foresaw their weddings.

Huy-Tuan was very lucky. His dad sent him out to sea with a group on a small boat for any land of freedom and he was only fourteen. After a couple days the boat capsized and all died except for him and another adult. He floated on the water eating tiny fishes he could catch when suddenly the South Cross spy ship saw him and plucked him up and brought him to a hotel in Singapore from where he could communicate with me through the Navy Postal system and came to live with us.

Both boys became electronic engineers and now work with good companies, have five kids bringing my third generation of Vietnamese Americans to twenty. My wish is to see some of them go into politics and participate actively in the political system of this country.

Sealing contract with 7-Eleven

Wedding TuanAnh-LeChi, 07-20-80

Wedding BichThuy-ThanhTung 10-80

Wedding ThanhHuong-AnhQue 10-26-83

Wedding MinhChau-NickNguyen

Wedding TuanTai-Margaret

Wedding HoangHuy-KieuAnh

Wedding HuyTuan-Shelley

Grand Family Reunion

With grand kids

A few grand kids around

Fully retired, the respectable taxpayers

CHAPTER EIGHT

VIII.- Things to remember

As said I had many unsatisfactory things in life. But then everything seems to be falling in place. Good fortune? Protection given by our ancestors? Always God and Buddha would know. Like when we just opened our Seaside store for business with a good reportage by the local newspaper, then that morning when I was busy doing my paper works in my office a very big man entered and with his rumbling voice asked my wife "I want to see Bob". With very much apprehension she called me out not knowing what would be the outcome. I rushed out and he gave me his big hand shook mine violently and said "I have the impression of shaking hand with Abraham Lincoln!" And then he showed me his huge muscled bicep adding "I have only this. In any case if you need me please give me a call".

In business I realized that doing charity work is a necessity because it not only gives you personal pleasure but it also helps growing your business, the secret behind the increase and development of goodwill. That was why we decided to participate in two main programs, the Muscular Dystrophy Association MDA and the March of Dime. Yearly a couple of months before Labor Day we put canisters on the sales counter asking customers for help. At first we did not really believe in the good heart of the working guys in dirty coveralls with hands blackened by grease and smut. But then we saw clearly that they opened their heart much better than those white collars in coat and tie.

One time I pitched my tent on the rooftop of the store and stayed up there for one week getting my bucket down and calling out for donations. The result was in that week I got a total of $8,000. for MDA.

Every year I was top MDA fund raiser and we were invited once to a five day cruise to the Caribbean on the Norwegian Cruise Line. On the last night we had the honor to meet Jerry Lewis and Mr. John Thompson flying out in a helicopter to be in a big barbecue with the whole group.

With the March of Dimes every year in April I joined the big Walkethon to raise money. The first time I did in a 20 mile walk in San Francisco with Minh-Chau and Huy-Tuan who just arrived from Vietnam after being plucked up from the sea by the Navy South Cross off the South Pacific water.

The walk was beautiful through so many nice areas of the peninsula and ended up in a stadium where a huge cake was cut for all participants to enjoy. During the next three times we walked in Santa Cruz up and down the spectacular shoreline and always having to beat the headwind in the return leg. My wife had joined in this third walk with my six year old grand child Christopher who at midway could not take it anymore and had to be in a military truck back to the finish line. And though he was dead tired he felt all happy being cuddled up the truck by a “GI Joe”.

The last four walks were in the Salinas area and they cut them short to 10 miles because so many people had quit mid way. I had retired after seven walks for which I had raised a total of more than $35,000. and we were hosted to a seven day stay in the famous El Coronado Hotel in San Diego in which we were entertained in a beach barbecue. We had the extreme honor to sit next to the famous Dr. Jonathan Salk the father of the Salk anti polio vaccine. Also we were treated to one week stay at the famous hotel Chateau de Fontenac in Quebec City on July the 11th (7-11) and we enjoyed a cruise on the Saint Lawrence river with dancing on the ship deck. Owing to those activities my stores sales went up to the roof and the combined sale for the two stores had reached a monumental 3 million a year.

As for tax at first the feeling was “how come they were so heavy” and I complained with an American friend. With a big smile he said “You have to be pleased to pay tax, because for those who could not make any money they would not have that honor”. It was such a sensible and fitting answer! Then he continued smiling :”Spend it before they took it away from you”.

That was why we partook in the many group trips with vendors and others business owners during conferences or trade shows. And after Caribbean cruises came Paris, London, Bangkok, Shanghai, Acapulco, Madrid, Hong Kong, Disney World, Cancun,…, business expenses not only good for your own selves but they helped developing your view in business very suitable to the growth and profit of your business.

During those trips we often were with a big group of a few hundred persons, either owners of other 7-Eleven stores or vendors. We often discussed personnel problems, the conflicting interests between franchisees and franchisor, and the impact of legal matters and business laws.

During one of the gigantic receptions in Las Vegas I had the opportunity to talk at length with Bill Ososki who had become Florida Division Manager. I asked him a question that was embedded in my head for a long time. "Why did he give me the franchise contract, why did he bet on a lame duck?" Then Bill told me that when he was fourteen he had narrowly escaped from Prague with his mother while the hordes of Russian tanks advanced to the city shooting and killing. And he knew that for those refugees having a certain background and being intent to work they would need just a little push to emerge in a society of justice, freedom, and under the rule of laws.

On another occasion my former boss at the shoe department of J.C. Penney came to see me at my Seaside store. He offered his cooperation because he wanted to retire Then I asked him how much cash he could have on hand. To my question he answered that he could cash out of his life insurance $5,000. Here was my reply "I do not need that kind of money. I just need somebody to go in and shoulder some responsibility with me". I never saw him back! After more than 25 years working for such a big firm and now close to the end of his life he only could count on such a small sum. That was the fate of so many local people, swinging their arms out of their reach and surviving with credit cards! That was why during one of those orientation meetings in Fort Chaffee the speaker had kidded that you have to avoid being wrapped in bills when you die. I had learned the lesson.

On the 23rd of November 1981 we became US citizens and when we hold the small US flag in our hand to swear full allegiance to the USA I felt not only happy but blessed. From now on I could forget my past with all the dirtiness and lowness to live as a peaceful middle class taxpayer with a strong and forceful voice in the community. I changed my name to Robert C. Trando. Trando is the joining of my father and mother's family names and Robert came from my admiration of Robert Taylor, just the same feeling of all young men during my time. Also, in business the practice being for first name calling it would make it easier for people to recognize me. And my wife had opted for the name Elizabeth because she admired Queen Elizabeth and Elizabeth Taylor.

During one get together with all former VNAF friends in Orange County one man sitting next to me asked: "Are you losing your root"? My answer was "I lost it long time ago when my father was hand carried by my grandma fleeing the flood and famine of 1897 and abandoning the native village of Nhi-Khe for Thanh-Hoa. Then they left North Vietnam for Saigon and after twenty years one more time we left everything behind to come here for a new life. But this time, almost thirty years in California, the roots had gone deep and the branches had born flowers and fruits, I'd not say that I had lost my roots".

Besides we only came after so many and after us there will still be others coming. And we all are really equal and together we help improving this promised land so that our children and grand children can be proud that their fathers and grand fathers were not parasitic of this society.

Writing this memoir my mind is always towards all my benefactors, be them still among us or had them left us for a higher plane. I talk of the late Robert Littlefield and Hal Kauffman, the late Colonel Carl W. Elder and his wife Alta. I must cite Pastor Ernie Lineberger, Larene Kauffman, Ed and Karen Barker, Bill Ososki, Greg Shankle, William Pittman, Cal Thimpsen, and so on who had helped make our life better and more meaningful.

For a conclusion I want to quote the teaching of Buddha saying that everything down here is a mirage, real and unreal. And I also could not forget to quote a phrase in the Bible "Vanitas, Vanitatum, Omni Vanitas" .

Walkethon, Santa Cruz, with Chris 1987

Caribbean Cruise, MDA

Ecole de l'Air revisited, with General Dumaz

Return to France, Montpellier

Reunion with Dr. Hong and family, Monterey

Brother Cam, his family wedding, Los Amgeles

Visit of brother Loc from Saigon, brother Thien and Ms Nho, LA

ABOUT THE AUTHOR

Robert C. Trando was born on March 28, 1922 under the name Tran-do-Cung. He grew up during a rather peaceful period of the Nguyen Imperial Court under the French administration, in a middle class family of teachers.

He went through all stages of the French school system, primary, secondary and superior education with outstanding results. Then during his years at the Hanoi French University he started to be exposed to the ideals of liberalism, freedom and patriotism.

The defeat of Occidental forces by the Japanese further nourished his pride to be Asian and then the spread of the Viet-Minh under the banner of independence for the country attracted him.

The atrocity of the calamitous famine of 1944-45 killing millions of Vietnamese also contributed to his hate of the French. During the French war he fought for a while in the student front line company until the unit was disbanded,

He became a spy agent under the code name Z-4 working in Hanoi and defected to go South to become director of sports in the Ministry of Sports and physical education.

Mobilized in 1953 he was sent to the French Air Academy of Salon-de-Provence to be trained as air mechanical engineer. Back home he very earnestly worked to give the Vietnam Air Force a sound and solid structural foundation for its technical system. There he witnessed the 1960 coup attempt by the parachutists, the bombing of the presidential palace in 1962 by the insurgent pilots Quoc and Cu. And in 1963 he participated in the coup deposing President Ngo-dinh-Diem.

With the military regime he was assigned various civilian jobs among them the notorious Commissariat General for Commodities distribution with the rank of secretary. Retired in 1974 with the rank of Lt-Colonel he witnessed the tragic exodus to freedom when the communist army advanced to Saigon.

Being the last one of the family to escape he made it out on the last USAF C-130 flight and was reunited with his family in Fort Chaffee, Arkansas.

The Saint Timothy Lutheran Church in Monterey sponsored him and his family and they relocated there since 3 July 1975. Starting as a shoe sale clerk at J.C. Penney with $2.65 an hour, he later became owner of two successful 7-Eleven stores and finally retired in 1997 at the age of 75.

His five children were married, are professionals and have decent jobs. They gave him fifteen grandchildren. Besides he sponsored two nephews from Saigon, raised them like his own kids, sent them to school and they are also professionals working now for good companies. They also are homeowners and have five children, raising the number of his third generation Vietnamese-Americans to a total of twenty. He hopes to see among those young native born budding Americans some going into politics and becoming active in the national political system.

$12.00

Printed in the United States
24287LVS00002B/319-426

9 781418 475505